Ben Wagstaff
Angus Butterfield

BHS Butterfield
The Complete First Series

BHS Butterfield

The Complete First Series

First Published in Print in 2013

SECOND EDITION

ISBN- 10: 1492972037
ISBN- 13: 978 – 1492972037

© *Ben Wagstaff 2013. All Rights Reserved*

This title was previously published as an e-book in August 2013.
All Rights Reserved. No portion of this book may be reproduced, used, utilized in any form or by any means, electronic or mechanical, including photocopying, recording or by any information retrieval system, without first obtaining written consent from the copyright holder.

BHS Butterfield was created and written by Ben James Stuart Wagstaff and co-created by Charles 'Angus' Saxon Butterfield.

All rights of production and copyrights of the screenplays and concept are held by Ben Wagstaff. Purchasing this book does not give you any rights whatsoever to produce any of the screenplays within, either in part of full for any reason, commercial or otherwise. For information on production please contact the copyright holder.

Contact: info@bhsbutterfield.com

This Book is Dedicated to

All those who have ambition

and dedication to get where

they deserve to be.

Important Information

This book and the screenplays within it may contain content which some readers may find offensive. At no point do we intentionally aim to offend anyone. We do apologise if you have been offended in anyway and respectfully ask that you remember that BHS Butterfield is a comedy series and the plots and jokes written within are for comical purposes only.

The contents of this book and the opinions of characters within the series are not the views and opinions of the writers or creators of the series or anyone associated with the series.

We recommend that this book is only read by a mature audience, and if you are offended by and of the contents, then you simply stop reading it.

Please DO NOT copy actions that the characters in the series and book do, they may not be safe.

BHS Butterfield is a comedy series and not an accurate representation of the NHS. The series is in no way associated with the NHS.

BHS Butterfield: The Complete First Series

BHS Butterfield: The Complete First Series

Contents

Introduction from Angus	11
Introduction	13
The Characters	15
Episode One: Welcome to BHS Butterfield	20
Episode Two: Inspection Day	50
Episode Three: Aussie Wit	88
Episode Four: Over 50's Night	126
Episode Five: Aussie v Kiwi	162
Series Two Episode Three: A Day for Love	198
Behind the Ideas	239
Future Plans	246
What we get Asked	248
The Conclusion	253
About the Creators	256

BHS Butterfield: The Complete First Series

BHS Butterfield: The Complete First Series

Introduction from Angus

Ben and I have always had a passion for writing comedy which is what initially drew us together to work on this project in the first place. By no means was this the first of our creative endeavors, we'd delved into various other projects and what not before, but they all went to shit like most of our ideas, probably due to my ridiculously slack nature, yet I don't vote for Mr Milliband which might seem strange given that.

Despite our other plans, as you've probably gathered reading this, I actually got my act together and really pushed through with this project. We started out creating it like a kind of mockumentary come sketch show, pulling the most politically incorrect and offensive scene ideas out of our heads as we could. In the style of good old British comedy.

I proposed to Ben we take the piss out of our great British industries and services, and then following a short chat, we decided the good old NHS would be right for this. It seemed fitting to highlight the likes of the NHS given the brilliantly successful times they're in of course. He agreed and thought this would be a brilliant idea.

We basically wanted to create this shambles of a hospital that had been moved into a residential property due to the tough economic times, and then add in a few insufficiently qualified employees.

We probably exaggerated it a bit too much but we couldn't resist.

The first characters we came out with were the two surgeons Chris and Jack, we wanted the double act to come across as typical med-school interns, lazy, inexperienced, crude and distracted.

They're a likeable pair and I thought they really complemented to the disorganized hospital set up we'd created.

BHS Butterfield: The Complete First Series

Overall I was pretty happy with how Ben wrote the series, I think that it finds the funny side to the touch economic times and the effects they have on our services, minus some of our outrageously politically incorrect dialogue in some places.

I thank you a lot on behalf of myself and Ben for supporting us in buying the book, I hope you can join us in finding humour out of taking the piss out of probably out countries most prized public services. Ish.

Angus Butterfield

BHS Butterfield: The Complete First Series

Welcome to BHS Butterfield

Hello, my name is Ben Wagstaff and I am the writer of this book, the BHS Butterfield series and also one of the creators, it was me that came up with most of the ideas for BHS Butterfield and created the plots and the characters, the other creator is Angus Butterfield, he wrote the introduction just before this bit, you should have already read it, if your reading this book the usual front to back way.

I reason that it would only be polite of me to begin this book by thanking you the reader for purchasing it, both myself and Angus are appreciative of your purchase, after all, we do both profit from it. We also hope you enjoy reading the series we created, particularly me as I know just how much work went into writing the series and putting this book together for you.

So, what is this book? It's BHS Butterfield: The Complete First Series, this is the print edition, by which I mean you are sat reading a physical copy of this book rather than on Kindle, which was where this title was originally released, and is also still available on.

There are some differences of course between this printed edition and the e-book Kindle one, mainly the introductions have changed, a few things have been removed and added along with a bit of re-ordering. It should be noted though that all the BHS Butterfield screenplays in the e-book edition are exactly the same as the one's you'll find in here.

BHS Butterfield is a sitcom which me and Angus created and I wrote, although he did initially agree to write two of the episodes himself, that was until we found out that he wasn't great at writing screenplays and the job was left to me instead.

The original basic idea was a joint creation between the two of us, however the episode plots and characters were my ideas, he simply approved what I wrote and told me if he thought something needed changing, more often or not, this was when I ignored him.

The sitcom is based in a British private hospital and the series follows the day to day running of that hospital along with the staff that work within it, primarily the hospitals Australian manager, Andrew Harris who is first introduced in 'Aussie Wit', the two hospital surgeons Chris Lister and Jack Halstead and the assistant manager Molly Hanson, there are of course many other staff who make regular appearances throughout the series.

This book contains the screenplays that were written for the first series, it's a series of five episodes, however you may have noticed that there are six in this book, the reason for this is because I had finished writing one of the series two episodes and decided to include it in the book.

That's it for my introduction and it's time to introduce you to the characters, but just before, once again, many thanks for your purchase.

BHS Butterfield: The Complete First Series

The Characters

Hospital Staff

Andrew Harris – The Australian Manager

We are first introduced to the character of Andrew in the third episode of the series 'Aussie Wit'. He is the replacement for the outgoing manager Anthony Young who is fired at the end of 'Inspection Day'.

This was a character that I wanted to come across as being someone who got on with his job but could also have a laugh while doing it.

In terms of relationships with the other hospital staff he has his romantic interests firmly with his assistant Molly Hanson. He also comes across to be good friends with the chef Biff Wellington and the two surgeons.

Andrew is based on a real person; this person is Australian comedian and comedy musician Andrew Hansen, a member of the comedy group 'The Chaser'. Somewhat off topic but I do recommend having a look on You Tube for some of the stunts the group has done, they are worth a watch.

Chris Lister and Jack Halstead – The Surgeons

The comedy duo of the series, Chris and Jack are the hospitals two surgeons who are often more than happy to use an excuse they can in order to get a few hours off, whether it's creating an advert for the hospital or going on a date with one of the more elderly patients.

Appearing in all episodes, these two characters are often the most comical and also responsible for all that goes wrong, mostly due to their lack of ability and common sense.

The names for these characters come from two historical surgeons and doctors, one being William Stewart 'Halstead' and the second being Joseph 'Lister'.

Biff Wellington – The Hospital Chef

If you can see the joke in the name then good on you. Biff is the hospitals chef however at times he also doubles up into other roles within the hospital such as a surgeon or doctor when the other staff are away.

His favourite disk to cook up for the staff is a-positive with a dash of industrial grade cleaner soup, whereas for the patients, sick and out of date eggs are the most common dish of the day.

Molly Hanson – The Assistant Manager

Arriving in 'Aussie Wit', Molly is a doctor at the hospital but soon becomes the love interest of Andrew, leading him to giving her a promotion to assistant manager rather quickly.

Often in series one she shows that she may also have feeling for Andrew, in 'A Day for Love' we see there is more than one side to Molly.

Julia Walker – The Matron

Julia is the hospitals resident bandage obsessed matron, often being the go to woman for advice and always there to treat her patients, with bandages.

Will Drew – The Doctor

BHS Butterfield: The Complete First Series

Will is the hospitals less than qualified doctor who spends less time treating his patients and more time questioning them. He is one of the pioneers in making Anthony lose his job.

James Larrey – The Paramedic

Good friend of Julia's and the hospitals paramedic armed with no ambulance, only a bike.

Adam Nichols – The Mourner

Adam is the hospitals mourner who can usually be found asleep on the bodies up in the hospitals 'mournery'/bathroom. He also doubles up as the cleaner to Jack and Chris's operations.

Zoe Lynch – The Doctor

The only staff member who takes her job completely seriously, arriving at the same time as Molly in 'Aussie Wit' she spends most of her time complaining about the other staff before resigning and being literally chucked out in 'Aussie v Kiwi'.

Sophie Lizcock – The Cleaner

The hospitals cleaner who gives the advice to Anthony in 'Inspection Day' that leads him to failing his inspection and losing his job.

Lizzy Cumming and Eva Knight – The Nurses

The female equivalent of Chris and Jack often doing even less work than they do.

Anthony Young – The Original Manager

Appearing in the first two episodes, Anthony is the hospitals original manager, who then loses his job following an inspection where all of the staff are against him. He later makes brief appearances in 'Aussie Wit' and 'A Day for Love'.

Non Staff

German Inspectors

Lukas Beckenbauer, Niclas Faust and Leonie Fenstermacher are the three German inspectors known as Surgical Analysts (S.A) from 'Inspection Day'.

Dave and Joyce Parkinson

These are the Yorkshire couple that appear in 'Aussie Wit', they make Andrew start to wonder just how hard it is to get rid of a Yorkshire man and his wife.

PC Saxon and PC Hardy

Appearing in 'Over 50's Night', these are the two policemen that arrive first at the scene and make it seem more like a 1940's black and white film.

Huihana Ngaruruku

Yes this name is not in English, it's in Maori. Huihana is Andrews cousin from New Zealand, and someone he is less than happy to see appear at the hospital one day.

Louise

Although not one of the most comical or popular characters in the series, Louise is certainly the one causing most controversy, although that's a story for another day. Louise is Jacks girlfriend who appears in series two.

BHS Butterfield: The Complete First Series

BHS Butterfield

Series One – Episode One

'Welcome to BHS Butterfield'

BHS Butterfield: The Complete First Series

Welcome to BHS Butterfield

Being the opening episode to not only the series but BHS Butterfield as a whole, it was the one where I wanted to show the audience just what the hospital is like, and what they can expect to see in the future episodes, so this episode mostly introduces you to the various characters and their personalities, particularly In the opening sequence which shows the staff getting ready for the day.

This opening sequence also shows the laziness of characters such as Adam and the sarcastic humorous comical nature of the two surgeons.

Character List – *in order of appearance*

Jack Halstead & Chris Lister	Surgeons
Lynda Young	Managers Wife
Anthony Young	Hospital Manager
Will Drew	Doctor
Lizzy Cumming & Eva Knight	Nurses
Julia Walker	Matron
Adam Nichols	Mourner
Biff Wellington	Hospital Chef
	Work Experience Kid
	Mother in Law

BHS Butterfield: The Complete First Series

FADE IN:

1. EXT. OUTSIDE FRONT OF HOSPITAL – EARLY MORNING

   We fade into a shot of the front of the 'BHS Butterfield' hospital building as the sun is beginning to rise early on a mid-summer morning.

   This shot continues for a few seconds before the theme music starts and the scene changes.

2. INT. SHARED FLAT – CONTINUOUS

   We are now inside the flat shared between the two surgeons Chris Lister and Jack Halstead and the two hospital nurses, Lizzy Cumming and Eva Knight. We are outside the door of one of the bedrooms.

   Both of the surgeons suddenly run out of the room together getting stuck in the door, they keep pushing and pushing until they manage to get through.

3. INT. HOSPITAL MANAGERS BEDROOM – CONTINUOUS

   We now cut to the bedroom of the hospitals manager. Where lying in bed with his wife, Lynda Young, is the current BHS Butterfield manager, Anthony Young.

   An alarm clock on the bedside table goes off, a few seconds later Anthony sits up, followed by his wife. He turns the alarm off before getting out of bed, his wife lays back down.

4. INT. WILL DREWS ROOM – CONTINUOUS

   We now find ourselves in the bedroom of the hospitals

consultant doctor, Will Drew. After a few seconds of the shot he wakes up, looks at the time on his clock then goes back to sleep.

5. INT. SHARED FLAT NURSES ROOM - CONTINUOUS

We are now back in the shared flat but are this time in the room of the two nurses, Lizzy and Eva. As there alarm goes off they sit up looking active and ready for the day ahead.

6. INT. MATRONS BEDROOM - CONTINUOUS

This time we cut into the bedroom of the hospitals matron, Julia Walker who is sat up talking to her husband.

6A. ----OMITTED----

7. INT. SHARED FLAT KITCHEN - CONTINUOUS

Back in the shared flat once again now but this time in the kitchen where Chris is watching over the toaster. Suddenly the toast fly's out and hits him in the middle of the face.

In shock he stands fully up quickly whacking his head on the the above cupboard.

Jack begins to laugh at him. Chris then pick up the toast and throws it at Jack who manages to catch it in his mouth before spitting it out, just as the kettle boils. Chris pick the kettle up and pours the boiling water onto Jacks feet.

After a few seconds delay Jack begins to feel the pain, he then goes to punch Chris in the face but he bends down to pick his toast up and Jack instead punches the wall.

Chris now stands up again and takes a bite of his toast.

8. INT. WILL DREWS ROOM -- CONTINUOUS

We go back to Wills room again whereas before he wakes up, looks at his alarm clock and goes back to sleep.

9. INT. HOSPITAL BATHROOM/ MOURNERY - CONTINUOUS

Now into the hospitals mournery, which is located within the bathroom of the building.

There are two bodies laid in the bath with the mourner Adam Nichols lying on top asleep.

Anthony walks into the room and begins to brush his teeth without taking any notice of what is in the bath next to him.

> ANTHONY
> You can go home at night you know.

> ADAM
> (without appearing to
> have woken up)
> Yeah, but you keep complaining that
> I'm late to work.

Anthony now begins to brush the teeth of the dead bodies in the bath.

10. INT. SHARED FLAT BATHROOM - MORNING - CONTINUOUS

Once again back to the shared flat, this time we are in the bathroom.

The room is empty until the two nurses walk in and begin to brush their teeth in a normal manor.

After a few seconds the two surgeons walk in, barge through the middle of the nurses, grab the toothpaste, fill their mouths and spit it all out, before wiping their mouths and exiting the room.

11. INT. WILL DREWS ROOM - CONTINUOUS

We go back to will's room again, whereas before he wakes up, looks at his alarm clock and goes back to sleep.

12. INT. HOSPITAL KITCHEN - CONTINUOUS

We now go to the hospital kitchen where we find the resident hospital chef, Biff Wellington, working on buttering a slice of toast.

Anthony walks in and gets himself a glass of water.

                ANTHONY
Do you know what you have to do for tonight?

                BIFF
   (sarcastically)
Yes. It shall be done as a banquet fit for a member of the Royal Family of Great Britain and the countries of the commonwealth New Zealand, Australia, Canada, Cook Islands etc.

                ANTHONY
   (not noticing the
   sarcasm)
Good! And there's no need to cook for any of the staff today, they'll

all be busy on a training course.

                BIFF
And what about the patients?

              ANTHONY
Just give them a potato each.

                BIFF
Right, OK then.

              ANTHONY
   (walking out of the room)
I'll speak to you later, I'm off to
go pleasure my wife.

At that moment Biff walks over to the fridge and pulls out a party sausage.

                BIFF
You'll be wanting your sausage then?

Anthony turns back to face him.

            BIFF (CONT'D)
Oh no, bit big to be yours.

The front door opens and the two nurses walk in prepared for the day of work ahead.

                LIZZY
Morning.

Lizzy and Eva now pick up a file each that are laid on the kitchen side and look inside them.

EVA
Looks like an easy day.

They now go to walk out of the room.

ANTHONY
Where are Chris and Jack?

LIZZY
Er.

EVA
They were right behind us.

The door opens again and the two surgeons rush in and grab their files.

CHRIS
(looking at his watch)
And not even late today.

JACK
Well, I guess there's a first for everything.

They now leave the room.

ANTHONY
(shouting to the two surgeons)
You know that you need to look after that work experience kid today don't you?

CHRIS (O.S.)
Yeah, we're always up for a day

off.

The door now opens again, entering this time is the matron, Julia, with her is the hospitals paramedic James Larrey and the cleaner, Sophie Lizcock.

As James and Julia hang their coats up, Sophie goes to get them their files.

                    SOPHIE
Morning.

                    JAMES
What time's that training today?

                    ANTHONY
One.

                    JULIA
What's it for again?

                    ANTHONY
Just general training.

The door opens once again and the Consultant Doctor Will Drew rushes in and trips over.

                    WILL
Sorry I'm late.

                    ANTHONY
Ah, Hello, you seem to spend so little time here maybe I should re introduce you to this place. This is BHS Butterfield.

13. EXT. OPENING TITLES - DAY

The show's opening titles begin by showing the full front of the hospital building. As the theme music begins the hospital staff begin to come out of the front door and form as though they are posing for a sports team photo. In the top centre of this formation is the manager. Once the full formation is complete the action freezes and becomes a sketched photo. Over this comes the 'BHS Butterfield' title card.

14. INT. DINING ROOM - MORNING

We cut to the houses dining room which usually doubles up as the hospitals surgery.

The table is currently set out for a meal however. The two surgeons walk in with patient one being carried between the two of them. They notice that the table is set out.

>   CHRIS
> Shit. We have operations to do
> here.

>   JACK
> Let's use the garden instead.

15. INT. HOSPITAL WARD - MORNING

We now go to the hospitals main ward which is located in a spare bedroom of the house.

Lying around on the floor is a number of sleeping bags, some with patients laying around on them. Some are sleeping where as some are sat up reading.

Lizzy walks into the room now, walks over to one of the patients, picks up a clipboard that is laid beside them, looks at it and begins tutting.

After a few seconds, Julia walks in to the room holding a large box of bandages, she then walks over to be next to Lizzy, she also looks at the clipboard and begins tutting.

                  JULIA
What's wrong with this one?

                  LIZZY
    (whispering to Julia)
Lung disease...

Julia now shakes her head and tuts for a few seconds before turning to the patient and smiling, the patient begins to violently cough.

                  JULIA
Don't worry yourself the slightest
bit dear, you just have a bad cough
that's all. Here try a bandage.

Julia now empties the entire box of bandages over the patient. She then turns back to Lizzy.

                JULIA (CONT'D)
I'll go get Adam.

They nod to each other.

16.   EXT. HOSPITAL BACK GARDEN - MORNING

Outside the back of the hospital in the garden now. Out of one of the back doors come the two surgeons still carrying patient one between them.

They walk out into the middle of the garden before dropping the patient.

They then kneel down and begin to look over the patient.

>   CHRIS
> So, any idea?

>   JACK
> Fuck no!

>   CHRIS
> Well. I'm going to use my expert
> knowledge and my trained eye here,
> and say, I think we're going to
> need to make use of the big knife.

>   JACK
> I have to say, I do agree with you
> on this matter.

Both of the surgeons now look at each other and nod before Jack stands up and walks back towards the building.

17. INT. HOSPITAL KITCHEN -- CONTINUOUS

We join Jack in the kitchen as he enters, also in the room is Biff who is preparing soup.

Jack begins to look around the room.

>   BIFF
> Are you wanting the 'big' one?

                    JACK
        Yeah--

Biff turns round to face Jack, as he does this he begins to pour disinfectant info the soup.

                    BIFF
            (pointing to a knife)
        In that Pie.

                    JACK
        Much thanks.

18.   EXT. HOSPITAL BACK GARDEN - CONTINUOUS

Straight back to the back garden now where Chris is not examining the patient with a rolled up piece of paper that he is using as a telescope.

Jack re appears from the house with a knife, he holds it up triumphantly.

                    JACK
        I've got it!

Chris now looks up and holds up the paper telescope in the same triumphant way.

                    CHRIS
        Ahh, perfect.

Jack now begins to walk towards Chris and the patient but he trips.

The scene fades to black before fading back into the scene.

The two surgeons are now stood up looking over Patient One who is covered in blood. They then look up and face each other.

                    CHRIS (CONT'D)
I think I know what's wrong. I can't be sure, but --

                    JACK
He was stabbed.

19. EXT. HOSPITAL BACK GARDEN - CONTINUOUS

Remaining in the back garden of the building now, but this time we are at the other side of the garden.

There is an outside table set up with a few chairs around it, sat on one of the chairs is patient two.

In the background of the shot is the two surgeons with a hose pipe clearing the blood from their patient.

Will Drew, the consultant doctor makes his entrance by sliding onto his chair, however he slides and falls over along with the chair.

He quickly gets back up trying to keep as much dignity as possible.

Once sat back up he places his briefcase on the table, opens it, takes a sandwich out of it, closes it, places it on the floor, takes one bit out of it, then throws it behind him.

                    WILL
You know, you look just like my

last girlfriend did.

              PATIENT TWO
Really, that's a coincidence, it happens a lot these days.

              WILL
Yeah-- mind you, she did look a lot better before that car hit her.

At this point the two surgeons in the background now have a sweeping brush and are hitting the patient.

              WILL (CONT'D)
So then, what's wrong with you?

              PATIENT TWO
Well, I sort of came here to find out, I thought you'd have a better idea than I would, it is your job after all.

              WILL
Yeah, very true that, but I'm afraid you'll have to tell me.

              PATIENT TWO
Well I don't really have any idea, surely you must have? You are a real doctor aren't you?

              WILL
Yeah of course, I spend all weekend traveling through time and space-

              PATIENT TWO

> (sounding confused and
> increasingly annoyed)
> Excuse me?

> WILL
> YES! I'm a real doctor, we just
> don't seem to be able to afford
> proper training anymore.

> PATIENT TWO
> (sarcastically)
> I do thank you for being so
> helpful.

> WILL
> Thank you, I do try.

> PATIENT TWO
> That wasn't a chat up line -- it
> was sarcasm.

> WILL
> I knew that-- How about you start
> with your symptoms.

At this point in the background of the scene, we see the hospital mourner, Adam walks out of the house and up to the patient and surgeons in the background. He helps them drag the patient away.

20. INT. HOSPITAL KITCHEN - DAY

Now into the kitchen where the room is now empty except for the chef Biff Wellington who is preparing soup in a pot ready for the nights meal.

He places his spoon into the pot then tries the contents, at first he appears satisfied with it, then he suddenly spits it back into the pan.

He then gets the salt and pours some into the pan, he then takes another sip and once again spits it back into the pan.

This time he pours all of the remaining salt into the pan and takes yet another sip, however he does not spit it out this time.

                BIFF
           (to himself)
     Just a little more flavour needed I
     think.

He now walks over to the fridge, takes out a large bar of lard then places it into the pan.

Now he walks out of the room, before returning a few seconds later with loads of medicines which he begins to pour into the pan

Finally, he takes off his sock and places it into the pan before taking one last sip.

             BIFF (CONT'D)
           (to himself)
     Perfect.

21.   10 SECOND BREAK UP SHOT #1

22.   INT. MANAGERS OFFICE - DAY

We now go to the office of the hospital manager, Anthony Young where we find him sat at his desk, opposite him is a social worker and Will.

> SOCIAL WORKER
> So what the story so far.

> ANTHONY
> Well, she was admitted last week after being beaten up by her father and his friends while they were drunk.

> SOCIAL WORKER
> And who has been treating her while she's been here.

> ANTHONY
> (pointing at Will)
> That would me Dr Drew here.

> WILL
> (casually)
> Hello.

> SOCIAL WORKER
> So does she have anywhere to go back to live?

> ANTHONY
> She's said she doesn't want to go back to live there.

> SOCIAL WORKER
> Well that is understandable, we'll find her somewhere else to live.

> WILL

>   What about with the Australian Rugby
>   team?
>
>   SOCIAL WORKER
>   What?
>
>   ANTHONY
>   Why would we send her to live with
>   the Australian rugby team?
>
>   WILL
>   Simple, they never beat anyone.

23. INT. HOSPITAL KITCHEN - DAY

>   Back into the kitchen where Biff is still preparing food for the night.
>
>   Chris and Jack walk into the room with the work experience kid that they are meant to be looking after for the day.
>
>   CHRIS
>   Right, this is where we keep the
>   chef, the food, and all out tools.
>
>   WORK EXPERIENCE KID
>   You keep all your surgery tools in
>   the kitchen?
>
>   JACK
>   Well, almost, there are one or two
>   in the garage as well.
>
>   BIFF
>   Do you have that knife from
>   earlier?

CHRIS
The big one?

BIFF
Yeah, need it to do the veg.

JACK
Left it out, I'll got get it in a minute.

CHRIS
Might need a bit of a wash though, It's got a bit of infected leg on it.

BIFF
No need to wash it, seasons the veg.

Jack walks up to the pan that is on the hob, he takes the lid off it and takes a big sniff.

JACK
Smells nice. Unusual for your cooking.

CHRIS
What is it?

BIFF
Stew. For later.

CHRIS
What is going on later?

BIFF

Anthony's got the mother in law
round. Cooking for them all.

At this, Jack spits into the stew and stirs it round. Biff
notices him doing this.

          BIFF (CONT'D)
I've already done that.

          JACK
Bit more flavour never hurts
anyone.

          CHRIS
I take it that's why we are all being
sent on a training course.

          BIFF
Probably.

          WORK EXPERIENCE KID
Hello.

          CHRIS
Hi.

          WORK EXPERIENCE KID
I am still here.

          JACK
Yep, we can see that, not blind.

          CHRIS
You weren't far off being that time
you walked in on Julia.

> WORK EXPERIENCE KID
> What am I meant to be doing today?

> JACK
> Well, you're here on work experience, so you're going to experience, the work we do.

The door of the kitchen opens and the hospitals mourner Adam Nichols walks in.

> ADAM
> You two wanted me?

> JACK
> Yep, and unusually it's not because Biff's cooking has killed anyone.

> ADAM
> What do you want?

> CHRIS
> Well this is the work experience guy. Need you to help him out.

> ADAM
> Sure thing.

> WORK EXPERIENCE KID
> Who's this guy?

> JACK
> Adam, he's the mourner.

> WORK EXPERIENCE KID
> Why do I need the mourner with me?

CHRIS
We do, comes in useful.

WORK EXPERIENCE KID
So what will I actually be doing?

JACK
Well, I think it's an amputation this afternoon, were both away training though, I'm sure you'll be fine alone.

24. INT. 10 SECOND BREAK UP SHOT #2

25. EXT. OUTSIDE THE FRONT OF THE HOSPITAL - AFTERNOON

It is now the afternoon and we are outside the front of the hospital where there is a mini bus waiting with some of the hospital staff assembled nearby, Julia, James and the two hospital nurses Lizzy Cumming and Eva Knight.

The front door opens and Chris and Jack walk out along with Anthony.

ANTHONY
Right, you're all of team building.

JULIA
Team building?

CHRIS
I thought it was a training course?

ANTHONY
No, it's team building.

JACK
Doing what?

ANTHONY
Paintball.

EVA
Does that mean the boys get to shoot at us?

LIZZY
Nice and hard.

ANTHONY
Yes, yes it does.

JULIA
Well they better not leave a mess on me.

CHRIS
And I take it you're not coming.

ANTHONY
No, too busy here.

JACK
Fuck that, if were going paintballing, you're coming with us.

ANTHONY
I can't leave the hospital.

Jack and Chris walk up to Anthony and grab him before dragging him into the minibus.

CHRIS
Ah well.

26. INT. HOSPITAL BATHROOM/ MOURNERY - AFTERNOON

We make a return to the bathroom where there are two bodies in the bath.

Standing next to the bath is Adam with the work experience kid.

ADAM
Right, this is the mournery where I work.

WORK EXPERIENCE KID
It's a bathroom?

ADAM
Yeah, we'll there's not much money invested into this place, have to improvise a lot.

WORK EXPERIENCE KID
Why do I need to see the mournery if I'm going to be doing surgery work experience?

ADAM
Because if your anything like Chris or Jack, most of your patients will end up in here.

Adam picks up a bag of ice that's at the side of the bath, he opens it and then begins to empty the ice over the bodies in the bath, at he does the top one begins to move.

                    WORK EXPERIENCE KID
          Did that one just move?

                    ADAM
          Shouldn't have? Used plenty of
          sedation on that one.

The body twitches, before the person sits up. Adam panics
and pushes it back down.

                    ADAM (CONT'D)
              (to body)
          I've told you already, we don't
          know how to do that operation.

27.   INT. HALL WAY - DAY

Into the hospitals main hallway. Facing the front door, we
see a figure appear at the door before a knock.

Lydia Young, Anthony's wife appears from one of the doors
off the hallway and answers to door, it is Anthony's mother
in-law.

                    LYDIA
          Mum.

                    MOTHER IN LAW
          Hello dear.

                    LYDIA
          How have you been?

                    MOTHER IN LAW
          Not too bad actually dear.

> LYDIA
> I'm afraid I'm not actually sure
> where Anthony's gone.

> MOTHER IN LAW
> Never reliable that man.

At this point Biff walks past.

> LYDIA
> (to Biff)
> Have you seen my husband anywhere?

> BIFF
> I think he got dragged off with the
> rest of them.

28. INT. 10 SECOND BREAK UP SHOT #3

29. EXT. PAINTBALL FIELD - AFTERNOON

In the paintball field where Julia, James, Eva, Lizzy, Chris and Jack are all armed and ready to play.

Also part of their group is Anthony, who has been given a gun and no armour.

A Whistles blows and the game starts.

1 MINUTE IMPROVISATION BY CHARACTERS

Chris and Jack now run into each other. They stop and hold their guns at each other's head.

> CHRIS
> I'll be honest, I'd rather point my

gun at a female.

> **JACK**
> Same.

> **CHRIS**
> What's your opinion on friendly fire?

Jack shoots him in the head.

> **CHRIS (CONT'D)**
> Okay, stupid question.

> **JACK**
> Where is Anthony?

> **CHRIS**
> That was the idea I had.

Anthony now runs past them, without him noticing they both follow, after a few seconds they both open fire on him from behind.

30. INT. 10 SECOND BREAK UP SHOT #4

31. INT. DINING ROOM - AFTERNOON

Into the hospitals dining room where the mother in law is sat along with Lydia. They are eating their meals.

> **MOTHER IN LAW**
> Will your husband actually be joining us?

> **LYDIA**

I'm sure he will be back soon.

From outside the room we can hear the front door open then close, a few seconds later Anthony appears in the dining room bruised and covered in paint.

                    ANTHONY
Sorry I'm late.

32. CLOSING TITLES

33. INT. DINING ROOM - AFTERNOON

The dining room again where this time Anthony is also sat down, still bruised and covered in paint.

Suddenly a body fly's across the table before falling off at the other side taking everything that was on the table with it.

We can see that it is Chris and Jack who have thrown the body.

                    CHRIS
It's an emergency.

                    JACK
Need the space to operate.

                MOTHER IN LAW
What is going on here?

THE END

BHS Butterfield: The Complete First Series

Note from the Writer

So that was episode one, the title for the episode is 'Welcome to BHS Butterfield' and I hope that it did welcome you to the series and give you an introduction to the characters.

This was probably the hardest episode to write, there are many many jokes and situations written for each of the characters, most of which are featured in later episodes, however as this is the first episode, the main focus has to be on establishing the characters rather than using content written around them.

There is no central story that takes place in this episode, instead there is a number of smaller plots that are incorporated into the episode, one being the mother-in-law of Anthony coming round to visit while the other is the staff training.

The opening sequence with little speech takes up a large portion of the episode. The intention of this opening is for it to have the feel of an opening from a feature length presentation, and in short to tell the audience that this is who these people are, this is what they are like and your about to see what they do.

You may have read this episode and thought there are parts that don't flow, you'll notice this more when you read the rest of the episodes which do flow much better. The reason for this is that a lot of the scenes for this first episode were taken from the original pilot script when the BHS Butterfield was still a sketch show, although I did re-write them to adapt to the sitcom style, they don't fit together completely as they should.

This episode is also unique in the series as it contains the one plot idea that Angus came up with, this being the work experience kid scenes, it's something he wanted to have added in right from the beginning.

BHS Butterfield

Series One – Episode Two

'Inspection Day'

BHS Butterfield: The Complete First Series

Inspection Day

Quite possibly the most offensive episode of BHS Butterfield.

Featuring the 3 surgical analysts' or S.A for short for Germany. If you had a read of Angus's introduction at the very start of this book, he sums this episode up in just one sentence 'We probably went a bit too far, but we couldn't resist'.

So this is the episode where we see the end of Anthony, at least as the hospitals manager anyway. We also see just what his staff think of him and a hint at what is to come with the man that replaces him.

Character List – *in order of appearance*

Jack Halstead & Chris Lister	Surgeons
Anthony Young	Hospital Manager
Lukas Beckenbauer	Lead Inspector
Niclas Faust	Inspector
Leonie Fenstermacher	Inspector
Biff Wellington	Hospital Chef
Julia Walker	Matron
Adam Nichols	Mourner
Sophie Lizcock	Cleaner
Will Drew	Doctor
Lynda Young	Managers Wife

FADE IN:

1. INT. HOSPITAL STAFF ROOM - MORNING

We start off in the hospitals staff room early on a summer morning.

Sat on each of the sofas is the two hospital surgeons Chris Lister and Jack Halstead.

> JACK
> I don't know what I'm doing wrong.

> CHRIS
> Well what lines are you using?

> JACK
> Hello.

> CHRIS
> Hello, is that really the best you can do?

> JACK
> Yeah, it's not that easy.

> CHRIS
> I don't even know why you keep trying, that pubs just a pick up point for rent a slag.

> JACK
> Because you're never in there are you.

> CHRIS

No I'm not, because unlike you, I use the right lines and can be shoving it up there within 5 minutes.

          JACK
So what lines do you use?

          CHRIS
I don't know, something different.

          JACK
Like.

          CHRIS
     (pointing at his face)
This face is leaving in 5 minutes, and you better be on it.

          JACK
Any more…

          CHRIS
By day I'm a surgeon and by night, I want you in my bed.

          JACK
I'll give it a try.

The door to the room opens and the hospitals manager Anthony Young appears.

          ANTHONY
I thought I told you two to take the day off.

Appearing behind him now is the lead inspector, Lukas Beckenbauer, and the two other inspectors Niclas Faust and Leonie Fenstermacher, all of the inspectors are German and wearing brown shirts.

> LUKAS
> And why would you ask two of your staff to take a day off on the day of your inspection?

> ANTHONY
> Ermmm.

> LUKAS
> Why would you ask two of your staff to take a day off on the day of your inspection?

> ANTHONY
> I can explain...

> LUKAS
> Can you?

> ANTHONY
> No.

2.   EXT. OPENING TITLES - DAY

The show's opening titles begin by showing the full front of the hospital building. As the theme music begins the hospital staff begin to come out of the front door and form as though they are posing for a sports team photo. In the top centre of this formation is the manager. Once the full formation is complete the action freezes and becomes a sketched photo. Over this comes the 'BHS Butterfield' title card.

3. INT. MANAGERS OFFICE – MORNING

We now go into the manager's office where Anthony is sat behind his desk with Lukas, Niclas and Leonie standing in front of him.

ANTHONY
Good morning, do take a seat.

LUKAS
Ve prefer to stand.

ANTHONY
OK then.

LUKAS
Let me intorudce for you. I am today's lead inspector, my name is Lukas Beckenbauer.

ANTHONY
Good morning Mr Beckenbauer.

LUKAS
Guten Morgen Mr Young. My two secondary inspectors today are Niclas Faust and Leonie Fenstermacher.

ANTHONY
Good morning Mr Faust and Mrs Fenstermacher.

NICLAS

Guten Morgen Mr Young.

LEONIE
Guten Morgen Mr Young.

LUKAS
I vill translate for you Mr Young.
I am Lukas Bowlmaker, and this is
Niclas fists
    (points at niclas)
Leonie Windowmaker
    (points at leonie)

ANTHONY
So Niclas Fists Leonie Windowmaker?

LUKAS
Vat is correct Mr Young. Ve are
surgical analysts or the SA for
short.

ANTHONY
Right.

LUKAS
Ve will be inspecting various parts
of your day to day operation.

ANTHONY
Right.

LUKAS
Do you understand all of this Mr
Young?

ANTHONY

Yes.

     LUKAS
Gut.
 (there is a phone ring)
Ah, this is the head of the SA, I vill be one minute.
 (he answers the phone)
Hallo mine fuhrer.... Yes ve have made it here. Yes ve will be conducting the inspection in due course. Gutten bye.
 (turns to Anthony)
Ve will start our inspection immediately.

4. INT. HOSPITAL KITCHEN - MORNING

We now go to the hospitals kitchen where the resident chef, Biff Wellington is preparing the patients breakfast. As we join the action he is looking in the fridge.

While he is still looking in the fridge when Lukas walks in and looks at him.

     LUKAS
Guten morgen Mr Wellington.

At this point Biff looks up holding a sausage from the fridge as a moustache. As he looks at Lukas he places his had up in the air as to wave and solute at the same time.

     BIFF
Good morning, to you to.

     LUKAS

Vas is this that you are doing?

He quickly throws the sausage behind him and puts his hand down, offering to shake Lukas's.

> BIFF
> I take it you're the inspector?

> LUKAS
> You are correct.

Lukas shakes his hand.

> BIFF
> Would you like to talk to me here or over the skies of southern Britain?

Biff laughs at his own joke.

> LUKAS
> Pardon.

> BIFF
> Sorry just a small joke.

> LUKAS
> I do not find jokes at all amusing.

> BIFF
> Clearly... So what exactly do you wish to inspect.

> LUKAS
> I need to start by inspecting the quality of the food you cook. I'll

begin by inspecting your sausages.

>BIFF
>(looking down at himself)
I still believe I have only one of them.

>LUKAS

Is this another one of your jokes?

>BIFF

Ye--

>LUKAS

I do not find any jokes at all amusing sir. I have just wasted precisely 3 seconds telling you this for a second time.

>BIFF

Sorry Jerry--
>(he says the rest of the sentence in a German Accent)

I do not vish to vaste your precious time any longer.

>LUKAS

Vis mocking, I do not find it--

>BIFF

At all amusing.

>LUKAS

Correct sir, can we continue the inspection now.

5. INT. HOSPITAL WARD - MORNING

Now to the hospitals ward where the matron Julia Walker is tending to some patients. As we join the action she is sat bandaging a patient.

Leonie and Niclas walk in and stand watching Julia without her noticing.

>   LEONIE
> Vat exactly is wrong with this patient?

>   JULIA
> Dead.

>   PATIENT ONE
> No...

Julia hits him in the face and he falls back down.

>   NICLAS
> Vight, and vat are you bandaging for.

At this point the hospitals mourner Adam Nichols walks into the room.

>   ADAM
> You wanted me.

>   JULIA
> Yeah, the usual.

>   ADAM
> Why do they keep thinking we can

give these sort of operations.

                JULIA
It's beyond me.

Adam now notices Leonie and Niclas.

                ADAM
I'm afraid you'll have to go, its not visiting hours.

                LEONIE
Ve are the inspectors.

                ADAM
Ah right, I forgot we were being inspected today, you're the surgical analysts?

                NICLAS
Ve are also known as the SA.

                ADAM
That's right.

                LEONIE
May I ask, vat is it you are doing with this patient?

                JULIA
As I have already told you, this patient is dead.

                LEONIE
But ve can see he is still breathing.

> NICLAS
> Vat is actually going on here?

> ADAM
> OK, if you must know, it's the managers idea.

> LEONIE
> Pardon?

> JULIA
> He says if we have any patients wanting operations we can't do then we should bandage them up and send them to the mournery.

> ADAM
> Exactly, that's what I'm here for.

> NICLAS
> Vight, vis is very interesting.

> LEONIE
> Indeed it is.

Both Leonie and Niclas make notes on their clipboards.

6. 10 SECOND BREAK UP SHOT #1

7. INT. STORE CUBOARD - DAY

We now to into the hospitals store cupboard which is located in one of the spare rooms.

This room is unorganized and looks like a typical spare room apart from boxes littering the floor. In the corner is a large box with the words 'JULIAS, You Touch and Ill Bandage You Next'.

In the room is Anthony who is looking through the boxes as the hospitals cleaner Sophie Lizcock walks in. She begins to tidy up some of the boxes.

                SOPHIE
What you doing?

                ANTHONY
Er, deciding which is the best drug to kill myself with.

                SOPHIE
Why?

                ANTHONY
Believe it or not, I'm planning on killing myself with it.

                SOPHIE
Fair enough.

                ANTHONY
So what are you doing here.

                SOPHIE
Cleaning up.

                ANTHONY
Why?

                SOPHIE
Because I'm the cleaner.

ANTHONY
Well I'm the manager but I don't do that very often.

There is a pause.

SOPHIE
So why are you wanting to kill yourself.

ANTHONY
Because, it's our inspection day, and I get the feeling that I'm going to lose my job, after all, all the staff hate me, although maybe I'm just being a little stupid.

SOPHIE
Na, you're not being stupid, of course they all hate you.

ANTHONY
Great, I'll be here for months to come.

SOPHIE
Where's your wife today?

ANTHONY
She's gone off into town to try find me a new job.

SOPHIE
She'll always be there for you.

ANTHONY

Just like I'll always come for her.

There is another pause.

Sophie now puts her arm around Anthony and begins to look like she has a cunning plan. As she does this the doorbell sounds.

              ANTHONY (CONT'D)
Did you just have a good idea, or did the doorbell just ring?

              SOPHIE
Both.

              ANTHONY
Someone else can get the door, what's your idea?

              SOPHIE
Well, you can make it look like you are a good manager you know.

              ANTHONY
And how do you propose that.

At this moment the door to the room opens and Biff walks in he begins to go through boxes until he finds a small tub of tablets which he picks up.

              BIFF
Sorry, just needed to get something to add some flavour.

He now leaves the room again.

                    ANTHONY
          Carrying on...

Sophie now goes to whisper in Anthony's ear. After a few seconds he begins to smile.

8.   INT. HOSPITAL KITCHEN - DAY

Were back to the hospitals kitchen now where Lukas is stood waiting for Biff to return.

Biff walks in carrying the tub of tablets that we saw him pick up in the previous scene. He walks over to a pan that is on the hob and begins to stir in the contents of the tub.

Lukas walks over and begins to look in the pan.

                    LUKAS
          May I ask vhere you store your
          ingredients?

                    BIFF
          In our store cupboard.

                    LUKAS
          And vhat else is in this cupboard.

                    BIFF
          Everything.

                    LUKAS
          Such as?

                    BIFF
          Bedding, drugs, you know,
          everything.

                    LUKAS
          You store your cooking ingredients
          vith your drugs.

                    BIFF
          Yeah, there often the same thing if
          I'm honest.

                    LUKAS
          You use drugs as your ingredients?

                    BIFF
          Yeah, it's the manager's idea.

     Lukas now makes some notes on his clipboard.

                    LUKAS
          Really? Vat is interesting.

                    BIFF
          Yeah, he said we shouldn't waste our
          drug stock, and just cook with it.

                    LUKAS
          Vight. Vell that concludes your
          inspection.

9.   10 SECOND BREAK UP SHOT #2

                                                        FADE IN.

10. EXT. PARK - AFTERNOON

     The scene now cuts to the middle of a park, early in the afternoon.

The shot if focused on two girls who are walking through the park talking.

CUT TO:

On the other side of the park we are with Anthony and Sophie who are looking at the two girls.

ANTHONY
Are you sure this a good idea?

SOPHIE
Yeah, of course, what's the worst that can happen.

ANTHONY
Well, If you're sure.

SOPHIE
Sure.

ANTHONY
OK, let's do this.

CUT TO:

We go back to the two girls now.

Anthony suddenly tackles one of them to the ground, knocking the other over in the process.

ANTHONY (CONT'D)
I think that's done it!

11. INT. HOSPITAL STAFF ROOM – AFTERNOON

BHS Butterfield: The Complete First Series

We now cut to the hospital staff room where sat on the sofa is Leonie and Niclas.

Laid out on the other is Chris and Jack, eating their lunch.

> CHRIS
> (with a mouthful of
> sandwich)
> So what did you say your names are?

> LEONIE
> I am Leonie Fenstermacher.

> NICLAS
> And I am Niclas Faust.

> JACK
> (also with a mouthful of
> sandwich)
> So what does that translate as then.

> NICLAS
> My surname translates as fists and Leonie's as Windowmaker.

> CHRIS
> (pointing at the two of
> them)
> So Niclas Fists -- Leonie Windowmaker.

> LEONIE
> That is correct yes.

Both Chris and Jack laugh to themselves.

>JACK
>That is very unfortunate.

>NICLAS
>Are you mocking our names?

>JACK
>Yes, that is correct.

>LEONIE
>We do not find it at all amusing.

>CHRIS
>Fucking hell, don't you Germans have any sense of humour.

>LEONIE
>That is correct.

At this point the door to the staff room opens and the hospitals paramedic James Larrey walks into the room.

>JAMES
>Call out.

>CHRIS
>Hold on a bit.

>JACK
>We want to finish our lunch first.

James looks obviously at the two inspectors.

>CHRIS

Right fine.

Both Chris and Jack stand up, place their fingers over there lips and walk out in a Hitler fashion.

>   LEONIE
>   They are mocking us again.

>   NICLAS
>   Quite right.

12. EXT. CONSULTING AREA - AFTERNOON

We go now to the outdoor consulting area, made up of a patio chair and table set.

Sat at one side of the table is the hospitals consultant doctor Will Drew. Sat behind him is Lukas conducting his inspection, throughout the scene he is making notes on his clipboard.

Sat at the other side of the table is Patient One.

>   WILL
>   (not really paying
>   attention)
>   Right, what the fuck is wrong with
>   you, make it quick, I want to go
>   home and watch the rugby.

>   PATIENT ONE
>   Excuse me?

>   WILL
>   Get on with it.

BHS Butterfield: The Complete First Series

PATIENT ONE
Right, OK then.

WILL
Quicker.

PATIENT ONE
Well, I woke up this morning.

WILL
As did we all.

PATIENT ONE
And I collapsed you see.

WILL
No, I'm quite sure I didn't see. I didn't get up until the afternoon for a start.

PATIENT ONE
Sorry can I continue.

WILL
I'd rather you didn't but if you must.

PATIENT ONE
Right, as I was saying, I collapsed.

WILL
Get on with it.

PATIENT ONE
I managed to get back up, but I

collapsed again around half eleven.

          WILL
Right and what do you want me to do about it.

        PATIENT ONE
Well I'm not sure.

          WILL
And neither am I.

        PATIENT ONE
You're the one who's meant to be a trained doctor.

          WILL
Na, I've got one of these internet degrees.

        PATIENT ONE
So what do you suggest.

          WILL
I'll tell you.
        (pointing towards the
        building)
Go in there, find a guy called Adam, he's our mourner, he'll sort you out.

        PATIENT ONE
But--

          WILL
FUCK OFF!

Patient One stands up looking offended and walks towards the building. Will now turns and faces Lukas.

> WILL (CONT'D)
> (casually)
> Well, how did I do then?

> LUKAS
> (looking shocked)
> Do you treat all of your patients like this?

> WILL
> Yep, standard practice, it's all Anthony's idea if I'm honest, and the bodies can be used for free heating in the winter.

13. 10 SECOND BREAK UP SHOT #3

14. EXT. PARK - AFTERNOON

We go back to the park now, where laid on the floor is the girl that Anthony ran into her, her friend is knelt down next to her.

Standing over them both is Anthony and Sophie.

James, Chris and Jack run up followed closely by Niclas and Leonie.

> CHRIS
> (to Anthony)
> You got here quick.

> ANTHONY

Well, I'm good at what I do.

CHRIS
Suspiciously quick.

ANTHONY
Well I do like to do what I do fast.

CHRIS
The only thing you ever do, is your wife and that's only because she likes party sausages.

JACK
Oooo, that's a good one.

CHRIS
And 100% true.

ANTHONY
We can argue about this later, now let's tend to this matter.

They now all look over the girl on the floor. Chris and Jack begin to examine the injuries, except the two inspections who watch over, throughout the scene they are making notes.

CHRIS
Right, what happened?

ANTHONY
She got attacked, thrown to the ground.

JACK
How do you know that?

GIRL TWO
It was him.

ANTHONY
Sorry, ignore her, she's just in shock.

GIRL TWO
No it was--

ANTHONY
I'll sort her out.

Anthony now takes the second girl of to the side.

CHRIS
Broken bone - arm.

JACK
Yeah, I think that's about right.

CHRIS
Quite a bad cut on there as well.

SOPHIE
I can sort that.

Sophie now takes out a bottle of disinfectant from her pocket and begins to clean the girls wound.

CHRIS
Sorry for sounding rude, but what the fuck are you doing here anyway?

> SOPHIE
> I came with Anthony.

> JACK
> Why? You're a cleaner.

At this point the girl wakes up.

> GIRL ONE
> Where is he?

> CHRIS
> Who?

> GIRL ONE
> That man, he ran into me.
> (pointing at Sophie)
> And you, you were with him.

Both Chris and Jack now look at Sophie.

> SOPHIE
> Anthony's idea.

15. EXT. CONSULTING AREA - AFTERNOON

We go back to the hospitals consulting area where Will is still sat talking to Lukas.

> LUKAS
> So let me get this right, vis Mr Young, he tells you to insult all of ve patients?

> WILL

                    Yeah, pretty much.

                              LUKAS
                    Why exactly is vat?

                              WILL
                    He says if we can get rid of them
                    the better, still charge them of
                    course.

                              LUKAS
                    Vell, vis is very bad practice.

                              WILL
                    Good point, I don't think he's
                    suited to being a manager myself.

                              LUKAS
                    I vill note that down.

                              WILL
                         (smiling to himself)
                    Good.

16.   INT. HALLWAY - AFTERNOON

      We are now in the hallway of the hospital where we can see
      Chris leaning up with his ear against a door and Jack laying
      on the floor trying to look into the room behind the same
      door.

      From within the room we can hear the three inspectors
      discussing their findings.

                              LEONIE (O.C.)
                    Vis place is a disgrace.

> NICLAS (O.C.)
> She is correct, this is not a place of care.

> LUKAS (O.C.)
> I have to say I agree vith you, all of the staff seem to be getting very strange instructions from vis Mr Young.

> LEONIE (O.C.)
> Is this the same Mr Young who injured an innocent girl just so he looked good for being there first?

> NICLAS (O.C.)
> Must be.

There is a phone ring.

> LUKAS (O.C.)
> Ah, it is Rohm. Hello Rohm, yes, ve have conducted our inspection. Yes, ve are currently discussing what action to take. Tell the fuhrer ve will report to him once ve are finished.

> NICLAS (O.C.)
> I think this place needs a change of manager, someone who can put some order in place.

> LEONIE (O.C.)
> Ves, I must agree there.

> LUKAS (O.C.)
> So it is decided, we let him go.

> LEONIE (O.C.)
> Very gut.

The door is now opened from the inside of the room by Lukas, Chris falls forward into the room.

> JACK
> Oi twat, that's my fucking head you just fell on.

> CHRIS
> If it makes you feel any better I think I've just broke my nose.

Julia comes walking out of another room and sees Chris and Jack on the floor.

> JULIA
> Do you boys want a bandage?

17. 10 SECOND BREAK UP SHOT #4

18. INT. HOSPITAL WARD - AFTERNOON

Now into the hospital ward where the only patient laying in the room is the girl from earlier, her friend is sat next to her.

Chris and Jack walk into the room with a cup of tea and a meal for the two girls.

> CHRIS
> You two managed to get our manager

fired.

                    JACK
          All the staff have agreed, we'll
          actually treat you for your
          injuries.

Adam walks into the room.

                    ADAM
          I heard we have more patients.

                    CHRIS
          We don't need you this time.

                    ADAM
          We not doing standard protocol?

                    JACK
          Nope, these two have got Anthony to
          fuck off finally.

Adam walks up to the girls.

                    ADAM
          Thank you so much.

                    GIRL ONE
          Anytime.

19. INT. MANAGERS OFFICE - AFTERNOON

Finally we are back to the manager's office. Sitting at his desk is Anthony. Standing in front is the three inspectors.

                    LUKAS

Vight, ve have thoroughly inspected your hospital and the day to day running.

ANTHONY
Have I passed?

LUKAS
I am afraid not Mr Young. Ve have no--

ANTHONY
But.

LUKAS
DO NOT INTERUPT ME MR YOUNG. Ve have no choice but to relieve you from your post of manager.

ANTHONY
But, you can't, I'll never be able to find another job.

The office door opens and Anthony's wife, Lynda, walks in with a pile of papers. She walks up to Anthony and kisses him on the cheek.

LYNDA
Hello dear, just been into the job centre, got you a meeting set up in the morning, they say there are a few posts which you may be suitable for, on a farm though.

20.   INT. HOSPITAL KITCHEN - AFTERNOON

In the kitchen is Biff who is serving up dinner for the staff. Will walks into the room and takes a sip of the meal.

>WILL
>Wow, nice taste, what have you put in it.

>BIFF
>Not sure of the name.

>WILL
>Ah right.

Will begins to walk out of the room again.

>BIFF
>It's a hypnotic drug though.

>WILL
>Really, what do they do?

Will falls to the ground and begins to snore.

>BIFF
>There a sleeping pill.

21. INT. HOSPITAL BATHROOM - AFTERNOON

Laying in the bath is the patient who was in the ward this morning. Sat on the toilet reading is Adam.

Adam stands up from the toilet and wipes his behind without any toilet paper.

Anthony walks in.

                    ANTHONY
            Hey Adam, I just wanted to say--

                    ADAM
            Good bye.

Adam offers out the hand he wiped himself with and Anthony shakes it.

22.   INT. HOSPITAL STAFF ROOM - MOMENTS LATER

Into the staff room where Chris and Jack are laid on the sofas. Anthony walks in.

                    ANTHONY
            Hey, I ju—

The two surgeons stand up. Walk over to Anthony and begin to push him out of the room.

23.   EXT. OUTSIDE FRONT OF HOSPITAL - CONTINUOUS

To the outside of the hospital where the front door opens, the two surgeons appear pushing Anthony, they push him out of the door and onto the floor.

                    CHRIS
            Goodbye.

They walk back into the building and disappear. After a few seconds Jack re appears and throws a suitcase out at Anthony.

                    JACK
            Goodbye.

24. END CREDITS

25. INT. HOSPITAL STAFF ROOM - EVENING

    We go back to the Hospitals staff room where Biff is sat drinking a cup of tea.

    There is a phone next to him that rings after a few seconds, he picks it up.

                    CALLER (O.S.)
        This is a reminder from a Mr A.
        Harris, QF flight 1 will be
        arriving from Sydney Australia into
        London Heathrow at approximately 3 in
        the morning.

                    BIFF
        Say that again?

    THE END

BHS Butterfield: The Complete First Series

Note from the Writer

Right from the pilot script, the idea for having an inspection was there, it just felt right. What was not originally planned was to have German inspectors known as the S.A, that idea came from a quick Facebook conversation with Angus, followed by a quick Google search to see if the word Analysts actually existed.

After knowing that the Germans would be the focus of this episode, I watched an old episode of Fawlty Towers for inspiration, I'm sure I don't need to tell you the episode. John Cleese as Basil Fawlty does in this particular episode pioneer the use of the Hitler walk in British comedy, so we had to rip it off, although for BHS Butterfield it's the two surgeons. After that we kind of went a bit far with the Germany references.

You may think we shouldn't be keeping this episode at all, however I think in the modern day, the offensiveness of the episode can be overlooked. Neither me nor Angus have anything against Germany.

For some reason, to write this episode, the dialogue for the German inspections was written with every W replaced with a V. I can confirm that this episode took hours and hours and hours to spell check.

BHS Butterfield: The Complete First Series

BHS Butterfield

Series One – Episode Three

'Aussie Wit'

BHS Butterfield: The Complete First Series

Aussie Wit

So this is the episode where my favourite character of all is introduced, Andrew Harris, the Australian manager that replaces Anthony. We also meet two new female doctors in this episode, the first is the female version of Andrew, and his love interest, Molly Hanson, and the second is the more serious Zoe Lynch.

As his first management aim, Andrew attempts to boost the hospitals publicity by launching an advertising campaign, with the surgeons taking the role of TV ad men.

Character List – *in order of appearance*

Jack Halstead & Chris Lister	Surgeons
Will Drew	Doctor
Andrew Harris	Australian Manager
James Larrey	Paramedic
Julia Walker	Matron
Zoe Lynch	Doctor
Molly Hanson	Assistant Manager
Biff Wellington	Hospital Chef
Sophie Lizcock	Cleaner
Adam Nichols	Mourner
Lizzy Cumming & Eva Knight	Nurses
Anthony Young	Original Manager
	Job Centre Worker
Dave Parkinson	Yorkshire Man
Joyce Parkinson	Yorkshire Woman

BHS Butterfield: The Complete First Series

FADE IN:

1. EXT. OUTSIDE FRONT OF HOSPITAL - MORNING

    We are outside the front of the BHS Butterfield building, early in the morning, looking out onto the main road that runs past.

    All we are able to see is the occasional car driving past, until suddenly the two hospital surgeons Chris Lister and Jack Halstead, come from either side and run into each other.

    > CHRIS
    > Oi, watch it, this is a new jacket.

    > JACK
    > All right. Calm down love, its only a jacket.

    The both begin to walk towards the building.

    > CHRIS
    > You know, I think we've just beaten our record, were only 10 minutes late today.

2. INT. HOSPITAL STAFF ROOM - MOMENTS LATER

    Laying on one of the sofa's is the hospitals consultant doctor, Will Drew, half asleep, he's been there all night.

    The door swings open and both of the surgeons enter, before throwing themselves on the other sofa.

> WILL
> (without making a move)
> You know the new managers arrived don't you? I had to pick him up from the airport earlier.

> CHRIS
> (he also does not move)
> What new manager?

The door opens once more and standing there straight in shorts and a t-shirt is the hospitals new Australian manager, Andrew Harris. He is wearing a stereotypical Australian cork hat.

> ANDREW
> G'day, the names Andrew.

Both of the surgeons turn round and stare at the new manager.

3. EXT. OPENING TITLES - DAY

The show's opening titles begin by showing the full front of the hospital building. As the theme music begins the hospital staff begin to come out of the front door and form as though they are posing for a sports team photo. In the top centre of this formation is the manager. Once the full formation is complete the action freezes and becomes a sketched photo. Over this comes the 'BHS Butterfield' title card.

For the opening titles for episodes three onwards, the original manager is replaced my Andrew.

4.   INT. MANAGERS OFFICE - DAY

We are in the newly redecorated office of the new Australian hospital manager.

The room is now littered with stereotypical Australian articles and props such as inflatable crocodiles, kangaroos and sharks.

On the back wall of the room, there are two flags, one is Australian whereas the other is a New Zealand flag with a large cross over it.

Sitting at the desk with his feet up and his hat still on is the Andrew. Facing him sat on the other side of the desk are the two surgeons.

> ANDREW
> Well, after that frankly poor performance, even worse than the New Zealanders, that, that old git before me did, I believe what this hospital need's is some bloody good advertising.

At this point both of the surgeons look at him, confused, especially as he gets up and walks over to a mini fridge in the corner. He opens it and takes out 3 cans of beer. 2 of which he throws to each of the surgeons before opening his own and taking a massive sip.

> ANDREW (CONT'D)
> So, I'm putting you two in charge of creating a TV ad, as well as that, that consultant guy is going to try a bit of mobile advertising.

JACK
And will you be doing anything?

ANDREW
Me, yeah, I'm of sprucing!

5. EXT. OUTSIDE FRONT OF HOSPITAL - MOMENTS LATER

The manager is now standing out at the front of the hospital wearing a red shirt, bow tie and straw hat. He has a megaphone and keeps pointing in random directions.

ANDREW
That's right ill people, come on in to BHS Butterfield, where you can have your self esteem massively and instantly reduced when we tell you just how ill you are. this is a massive operation clear out and all of out medicine stock has got to go. That's right a huge huge huge amount of organs ready to be transplanted and they all have to go by midnight tonight. It's total and absolute madness what offers I am offering you, in fact I think I need mental treatment myself.

Suddenly a car drives past through a puddle on the road, throwing water up and soaking him.

ANDREW (CONT'D)
I do believe my tempter has been massively increased.

6. INT. HOSPITAL STAFF ROOM - DAY

Sitting on the sofa is the only person in the room, she is the hospital matron, Julia Walker.

Although she is alone, there is however 'sitting' on the other sofa, one of the managers many inflatable crocodiles wearing his cork hat. The paramedic, James Larrey, walks into the room and sits next to the crocodile. He turns to it.

> JAMES
> You suffering from a hangover as well mate?
> (there is a pause)
> I thought you'd be snappy to answer to be honest.

> JULIA
> Do you have any idea where anyone is today?

James thinking that it is the crocodile speaking jumps up in surprise. He then faces the matron.

> JAMES
> Will you not do that please, I've already been to the toilet twice today.

> JULIA
> Surprising, I thought you normally went at the bottom of the garden or in the corner of the room.

There is no reply.

> JULIA (CONT'D)
> As I was saying, do you know where anyone is?

> JAMES
> There all doing these ad campaigns.

> JULIA
> What about the patients?

> JAMES
> It's up to whoever is left. I think Biff is working on surgery, and I'm consulting.

> JULIA
> Why don't we just give all of the patients bandages, that way we can have the day off.

> JAMES
> Has anyone told you that bandages are not the cure to every single disease or illness.

> JULIA
> I didn't mean use them to treat anyone, I meant use it to shut them up.

7. EXT. TOWN CENTRE - DAY

We are now in the local town centre where we can see Will,

he is walking around wearing a t-shirt the phrase 'BHS Butterfield- where your health comes first' written on it with a marker pen.

He is walking up to strangers and handing them leaflets as they walk past.

8. INT. HOSPITAL WARD - DAY

The hospital ward is current patient free. However instead there are the two surgeons and a woman they are using for their advert in the room.

They are currently working on filming there advert. Chris is holding a camera whereas Jack is in front of it with the woman.

CUT TO: VIEW THROUGH VIDEO CAMERA

                CHRIS
And action.

Jack and the woman are standing next to each other, with only one of Jacks arms visible.

                JACK
    Here at BHS Butterfield, we do value your health, and we never have any patient fatalities like this.

The woman falls to the floor.

CUT TO: NORMAL CAMERA VIEW

                CHRIS

>   What the hell did you just do?
>   (poking her with his
>   foot)
>   I think she might actually be
>   dead.

Jack now holds up an empty syringe.

>   JACK
>   I just found it in the bin, I
>   thought it might be useful for
>   this.

>   CHRIS
>   Right then, well best not to
>   dwell on the past.

At that moment, the new female doctor, Zoe Lynch walks in, however both surgeons are facing the other way and do not notice her entrance.

>   ZOE
>   Er, hi... have either of you
>   seen the manager anywhere?

Both of the surgeons now look round.

>   JACK
>   Do you want help carrying them?

>   ZOE
>   Sorry?

>   CHRIS
>   Well, it's getting hot in here,
>   do you want help taking some of

that off?

>   ZOE
> What?!

At this point both of the surgeons faint and fall on the ground.

9. EXT. OUTSIDE HOUSE - DAY

We are outside the house of a member of the public. There is no one around until Will appears in the fashion of a door to door salesman.

He knocks on the door and waits. When the houses resident answers he breathes over his face then hands him a 'BHS Butterfield' leaflet.

10. INT. KITCHEN - DAY

We now take a visit to the hospitals kitchen. The only person here is the hospitals resident chef, Biff Wellington.

He is reading his recipe book while mixing the contents of a pan.

On the worktop next to him are two livers.

The hospitals cleaner, Sophie Lizcock walks into the room carrying a bottle of disinfectant. Biff takes this bottle of her before emptying the entire contents into the pan and throwing the empty bottle behind him.

>   SOPHIE
>   (looking into the pan)

So what are you cooking today?

BIFF
Pig liver in... Er... brown.

SOPHIE
Sounds... nice.

BIFF
I'm having to do something quick today, I don't have loads of time, you know, with having to do all of this surgery work as well.

SOPHIE
And how is that going?

BIFF
Er, quite well so far. Well I mean it's only a transplant. I'm almost finished in fact.
>   (he pick up one of the livers)

Just have to pop the new liver in.
>   (He places it into the pan)

And then solder the skin up.

The two surgeons walk in with their camera.

BIFF (CONT'D)
Is there much difference between a human and a pig liver?

CHRIS
Have you got them mixed up?

BIFF
Yes, I do believe so.

Chris now looks into the pan.

CHRIS
Just do what we do... improvise.

JACK
To be honest, don't worry about it, as long as it tastes nice anyway.

11. 10 SECOND BREAK UP SHOT #1

12. INT. MANAGERS OFFICE - DAY

We go back to the manager's office now, whereas last time he has his feet up and his cork hat on.

Sitting at the other side of the desk is Zoe, the new female doctor, she is sat upright, looking professional on her first day of work.

ANDERW
So, are you new here then?

ZOE
Yes, only just arrived here.

ANDREW
I'm afraid I can't be much help then, I've only been working

> here since 6 this morning
> myself. So have you met anyone
> yet?

> ZOE
> Yes, a couple of people with a
> camera, I'm not quite sure who
> they are though.

> ANDREW
> Oh yeah, our surgeons. Yeah
> there working on an advert today
> so you probably won't see much of
> them.

At this moment, yet another new female doctor enters the room, Molly Hanson unlike the first, she is more relaxed much like many of the other hospital staff.

> MOLLY
> Hi, Er, is this the right place?

> ANDREW
> And you are Molly?

> MOLLY
> Yeah.

> ANDREW
> Welcome, this is Er,
>   (pointing at Zoe)
> I don't know actually.

> ZOE
> (turning and shaking
> hands with Molly)

Zoe, Zoe Lynch.

ANDREW
That's it. So you two are our two new doctors.

MOLLY
Yes.

ANDREW
Well, there's not really much you can do today, so I suggest just relaxing.

13. EXT. BACK GARDEN - DAY

We are in the hospitals back garden, where the two surgeons are once again working on their advert. However they are filming dangerously close to a paddling pool set out on the grass.

CUT TO: VIEW THROUGH VIDEO CAMERA

CHRIS (O.C.)
Here at BHS Butterfield, our staff always rush to any emergency, no matter what time of day.

Jack now runs towards the camera as though to show the 'rushing' of the staff.

However as he runs past the pool he trips, slips and falls into the pool and disappears from view. A few seconds later he re appears standing up, soaked.

CUT TO: NORMAL CAMERA VIEW

> JACK
> (holding up a
> inflatable crocodile)
> I know that he's Australian, but
> this is ridiculous.

14. EXT. OUTSIDE HOUSE - DAY

We join the Will once again outside a different house. As before he enters the shot in the fashion of a door to door salesman.

He knocks on the door and waits. When the houses resident answers he coughs over their face then hands him a 'BHS Butterfield' leaflet.

15. INT. HOSPITAL STAFF ROOM - DAY

Many of the hospitals staff are sat in the staff room, sat on one sofa is Julia, James and Biff. Sat on the other is the two nurses, Lizzy Cumming and Eva Knight, and Zoe. Sat on the floor is Molly.

The door opens and Andrew walks in, as he does this Molly stands up.

> ANDERW
> Right then.

> MOLLY
> Hi.

> ANDREW
> Hi... right, were going to help

with this advert.

16. EXT. HILL - DAY

We are now at the top of a steep hill where the two surgeons are giving a briefing to Andrew, Zoe, Molly, the two nurses, James, Julia and Biff, about what they need to do.

> CHRIS
> We're going to demonstrate that were all really quick at responding to an emergency.

> JACK
> Yes, we've already tried it once, but it didn't go well.

> CHRIS
> And we thought that it would be best to have everyone in it.

> ANDREW
> So what would you like us to do?

> JACK
> Well at the bottom of this hill we have a volunteer to act as our patient. We are all going to run to them and treat them as quick as possible.

CUT TO: VIEW THROUGH VIDEO CAMERA

We now go to the view through the camera, showing the staff of the hospital lining up ready. The advert starts on the injured patient at the bottom of the hill, the two surgeons are doing the voice over.

> CHRIS
> Wherever your injured, our large skilled team will be with you in minutes. Even the chef.

At this the action cuts to the staff at the top of the hill who all begin to run down the hill.

Andrew throws his boomerang with a bandage on towards the patient. The boomerang hits James in the back of the head knocking him over, as he begins to roll down the hill Biff trips over him.

As the two of them carry on rolling down the hill, they Knock everyone else over as though there bowling pins.

Andrew and Molly are the only two left standing, until the Andrew runs into a member of the public who is on a walk, this knocks them both over and along with everyone else except for Molly, they end up piled on top of each other on the patient.

As Andrew begins to sit up, molly who is still currently running down the hill trips and lands on top of him.

> ANDREW
> Right in the didgeridoo.

Andrew once again sits up, but this time his boomerang hits him in the face, and he falls back down.

> ANDREW (CONT'D)
> Ow.

                    BIFF
            (holding up a spatula)
        Do we have any need for this?

17. INT. HOSPITAL WARD - DAY

The camera moves across the room showing all of the hospital staff, from the previous scene, excluding the two surgeons, laying on the floor, recovering.

18. 10 SECOND BREAK UP SHOT # 2

19. INT. JOB CENTRE OFFICE - DAY

A back office of the local job centre is out next location where we join the old hospital manager, Anthony Young is being interviewed for a potential new job.

                JOB CENTRE WORKER
        Who did you say you were again?

                    ANTHONY
        Manager.

                JOB CENTRE WORKER
        And your first name?

                    ANTHONY
        Hospital.

                JOB CENTRE WORKER
        Mr Hospital Manager?

                    ANTHONY
        Yes.

BHS Butterfield: The Complete First Series

JOB CENTRE WORKER
Right. Are you sure about that?
It's just, that isn't the name
you have previously given us?

ANTHONY
Oh, you want my name?

JOB CENTRE WORKER
Yes, that is what I asked for.

ANTHONY
Sorry, I just got confused
because I'm a hospital manager,
I thought you were asking who I
was.

JOB CENTRE WORKER
Who you are, is your name?

ANTHONY
Is it? My name is Anthony, last
name young.

JOB CENTRE WORKER
Moving on. What have you
previously done as a job?

ANTHONY
Well I've done my wife plenty of
times, but it's usually her that
does the jobs.

JOB CENTRE WORKER
Right.... so do you have any
hobbies outside of work?

                        ANTHONY
        Well... I do like to gate crash
        funerals, then find vulnerable
        young women and tell them I can
        make them feel better and all
        warm inside.

                    JOB CENTRE WORKER
        And what does that involve
        exactly.

                        ANTHONY
        Well, normally my penis.

At that moment Will Drew appears and goes up to Anthony's face, breathes and coughs on it, then licks it before handing him a leaflet.

20.   INT. HOSPITAL ENTRANCE HALL - DAY

Biff Wellington is walking through the entrance hall of the hospital when suddenly the front door fly's open and a man runs in looking panicked.

                          MAN
        Please, someone come quick. My
        wife, I can't get her inside in
        time, I think, I think she's
        going to give birth in the car.

Andrew sticks his head out of the staff room.

                        ANDREW
                    (to Biff)
        Well, go on then.

                    BIFF
        Right.

Biff rushes out of the door tripping as he goes. We can only see Andrews head from the staff room but we can hear what is happening outside.

At first we hear a car door open.

                    BIFF (CONT'D) (O.C.)
        Please, don't panic, I'm a fully
        trained chef.

                    WOMAN (O.C.)
        You're what?

                    BIFF (O.C.)
        Please, keep still.

                    WOMAN (O.C.)
        What they hell are you doing?

                    BIFF (O.C.)
        We'll have to deliver here, we
        haven't got time to get you
        inside.

                    MAN (O.C.)
        Excuse me, my wife's in this
        car.

                    BIFF (O.C.)
            (pausing first)
        Oh fuck.

                    ANDREW

> Why am I starting to get the
> feeling that he is the wrong
> person to stand in for surgeons.

Biff walks back in.

> BIFF
> Wrong car.

> ANDREW
> Are you used to going into the
> wrong thing when there's a woman
> involved?

21. INT. DRUG STORE ROOM - DAY

We are in the hospital store room. The room is un organized and there are boxes everywhere. Sophie the cleaner, walks in and begins to tidy up the boxes.

As she is putting things into boxes she picks up a tub of tablets and looks at them.

> SOPHIE
> I don't think I've tried these
> before.

22. INT. MOURNERY/ BATHROOM - DAY

Andrew walks into the bathroom as any normal person would, he looks in the bathtub to see two dead bodies with the mourner, Adam Nichols, laid on top of them. He is shocked when he sees this.

> ANDREW
> (shouting out)

Why are there three dead bodies in the bath?

                CHRIS (O.S.)
There should be two.

                ANDREW
               (shouting out)
Nope, there are three.

                CHRIS (O.S.)
Try poking the top one.

Looking puzzled, Andrew pokes Adam, nothing happens, he pokes him again but this time harder. Adam wakes up and looks up at the manager.

                ADAM
Sorry, just having a nap...
Please do carry on and have a good shit.

                ANDREW
Crikey.

23.   10 SECOND BREAK UP SHOT # 3

24.   INT. HOSPITAL STAFF ROOM - LUNCH

It is lunch time in the staff room now, but it is empty except for the two surgeons who are sat looking out of the window.

                CHRIS
So many good ideas we had.

JACK
And not one worked...

CHRIS
We just need to hit on that one good idea.

JACK
Such as.

CHRIS
I'm trying to think.

JACK
Don't think too hard... you're not used to it.

As the Chris goes to hit Jack they hear a fast response ambulance go past outside. At that moment they turn to each other and in unison say;

CHRIS   JACK
Got it

They go to walk out of the room as Molly walks in and sits down with her lunch. A few seconds later Andrew walks in with his lunch and sits next to her.

The both sit eating their sandwich in unison. Then also in unison they take a drink.

ANDREW
(in a high pitched voice)
So, how's your lunch.

MOLLY
Fine thanks... and yours?

ANDREW
Fine thanks.

MOLLY
So, do you have any plans for the weekend then?

ANDREW
Well, I was going to ask you the same thing...

MOLLY
Really.

At this moment Zoe walks in with her lunch and sits in between them.

ANDREW
Anyway I'm watching the rugby.

MOLLY
Same.

ZOE
It's not a suitable place to be talking about watching men play with their balls.

In unison all three take a bite of their sandwiches.

Biff now walks in but doesn't sit down.

BIFF

> Anyone speak Yorkshire?

> ANDREW
> What do you mean Yorkshire...? I think its English.

> BIFF
> I mean Yorkshire...

25. INT. HOSPITAL ENTRANCE HALL - CONTINUOUS

> Biff leads Andrew into the entrance hall where standing by the door is the typical example of a Yorkshire man, Dave Parkinson, in a flat cap with a walking stick.

> DAVE
> (emphasis on all t's)
> Ah, abou't t'ime, someone t' came t' see me.

> ANDREW
> (to Biff)
> I see what you mean.

> BIFF
> So you don't speak Yorkshire then?

> ANDREW
> Na mate...

> DAVE
> Blood hell, I've t' been here for t' blood ages. I'm a Yorkshire man don't you know. I don't like t' be kept wai'ting

a't all.

                ANDREW
Alright mate.

                DAVE
Oh no, no't a blood Aussie, bunch of criminals you are. From t'hat rock of a prison.

                ANDREW
What?

                DAVE
You t'wa's t'hinking your better at blood cricke't than us Yorkshire men, I played for Yorkshire don't you know.

At this moment Zoe walks in and goes to Dave.

                ZOE
Eh up. Wha'ts t' wrong then.

                ANDREW
And since when were you Yorkshire.

                BIFF
I'll double that.

Zoe carry's on without noticing them.

                ZOE
Wha't can we do for you then.

> DAVE
> Ah, a proper woman. Well you t' see t'. I got up this morning to go buy t' Yorkshire paper, and I then went home and has t' Yorkshire brew while my wife wen't out with her friend Barbara across the road, theyv'e known each other for years you see. Anyway I t' fell when I was getting up t' go spend t' penny. So I t' came here.

> ZOE
> OK then sir, We'll get you sa't down and ge't a doctor t' come and see you.

Zoe leads Dave through into the staff room while Andrew and Biff look confused. As Zoe goes past Andrew.

> ANDREW
> By the way Zoe.

> ZOE
> Yes.

> ANDREW
> If he dies while he's here, I'll keep the ashes. Then Australia can have 2 sets next year.

26. INT. OUTSIDE HOUSE - AFTERNOON

It is early afternoon and we are once again outside a member of the public's house.

BHS Butterfield: The Complete First Series

This time there is a man who is tending to his garden as Will walks up to him, this time he sneezes on him then passes him a 'BHS Butterfield' flyer.

The man drops the flyer then turns around and punchers Will in the face making him fall to the ground.

27. INT. HOSPITAL STAFF ROOM - AFTERNOON

We are back in the staff room where Dave the Yorkshire man is sat on his own with a tea.

Andrew walks into the room and begins to walks around before stopping and 'ar'ing like an old man. This continues for about ten seconds before Biff walks in and begins to join him.

>   DAVE
>   (angrily)
>   Are you mocking me son.

>   ANDREW
>   No, were just talking in a
>   language you may understand.

>   DAVE
>   Watch it you blood criminal, I
>   may be old but I can still swing
>   a punch.

>   BIFF
>   Well i't like t' see tha't.

>   DAVE
>   If it was up t' me i'd have you
>   both out of this country.

>   BIFF
> But I'm t' British like you.
>
>   DAVE
> Yeah, but I'm t' Yorkshire.

Suddenly there is a car screech outside.

CUT TO:

28.   EXT. OUTSIDE FRONT OF HOSPITAL - CONTINUOUS

We are suddenly outside the hospital where the two surgeons are sat in the front of a car. An old woman, Joyce Parkinson, is lying on the road in front of the car.

>   CHRIS
>   (from inside the car)
> Oops.
>
>   JACK
>   (from inside the car)
> I don't think that idea worked
> that well.

Both of the surgeons get out of the car as Andrew comes out of the building. He goes to the old woman to try help her up.

>   ANDREW
> Are you OK?
>
>   JOYCE
> Go away you Australian criminal.
>
>   ANDREW

>   (walking away)
>   It's fine just leave her.

Julia now runs out of the house throwing bandages at Joyce.

>   JULIA
>   It's OK, I have the bandages.

The two surgeons now begin to examine her.

>   CHRIS
>   I think it's a broken leg.

>   JACK
>   I'd say both.

Out of nowhere Will appears and advertises a flyer to Joyce.

>   WILL
>   Can I recommend one of our many operations.

>   JOYCE
>   I only came to see, if my husband was OK, and I get treated like this.

>   ANDREW
>   (turning back round)
>   If you mean that old git inside, he's fine, I was just about to break his legs in fact.

29. 10 SECOND BREAK UP SHOT # 4

30. INT. HOSPITAL WARD - AFTERNOON

Lying next to each other is Dave and Joyce both are recovering.

DAVE
That bloody t' Australian.

JOYCE
Who does he think he is?

DAVE
He shouldn't be working in t' hospital t'all.

JOYCE
He should be in prison instead.

The two hospital nurses walk in with bandages, they walk up to Joyce and Dave and put the bandages in their mouths so that they can't talk.

LIZZY
Special request from the manager.

31. INT. MANAGERS OFFICE - EARLY EVENING

Sitting as usual at the desk is Andrew with his feet up and his hat still on. However this time there is another chair next to him, this chair is filled up by another of the many inflatable crocodiles, wearing his sprucing hat. Facing them is the two surgeons. They are all looking at the TV screen as the adverts come on showing the new BHS Butterfield ad.

32. EXT. OUTSIDE FRONT OF HOSPITAL - CONTINUOUS

We are outside the hospital looking through the surgeons small video camera. As they come running out of the hospital and to the car we can hear the voice over from Chris.

              CHRIS (V.O.)
Our top staff always rush to any emergency.

They drive out of the driveway and onto the road where we hear a screech.

              JACK
Er I think we hit her.

              CHRIS
Agreed.

              JACK
Shit, were still filming.

              CHRIS
Er think fast...

              JACK
Yes that's right, no matter where the thing is, we'll be there.

              CHRIS
We're there already.

33.   INT. MANAGERS OFFICE - EARLY EVENING

Andrew turns of the TV and turns to face the two surgeons.

ANDREW
You know boys. I'm not overly sure that thing advertising thing has gone that well.

CHRIS
It wasn't all that bad, you have people phoning up for discount operations and we've caused someone to need one of those operations.

JACK
Yeah, and we do have a new successful-Ish advert.

There is a long pause while everyone looks at each other.

ANDREW
Anyway I think we can call it a day. There is going to be no more ad campaigns while I'm here.

He takes his sprucing hat from the top of the crocodile next to him then puts it over his normal hat. He then stands up.

ANDREW (CONT'D)
Right then, see you tomorrow, I'm of sprucing.

At this he leaves the room. Leaving the two surgeons looking confused.

BHS Butterfield: The Complete First Series

34. END CREDITS

35. EXT. OUTSIDE FRONT OF HOSPITAL - EARLY EVENING

As before in the morning, Andrew is standing out at the front of the hospital wearing a red shirt, bow tie and straw hat. He has his megaphone out and keeps pointing as he talks.

>   ANDREW
> That's right, come on in to where you can forget about curing illness, with our fees this high, we'll make you sick! Bring your mother, bring your children, and bring your bed because you won't get one in here. That's right you'll be needing extra treatment for the heart attack you have when we bill you. We have tripled our prices so that I can have a bigger bonus at the end of the year. That's right come on in to BHS Butterfield.

THE END

BHS Butterfield: The Complete First Series

Note from the Writer

This is another episode which took a while to spell check, thanks to the couple from Yorkshire, for some reason the way I thought would be best to write their speech was to just add t' at the start of everything.

This was the first episode that I wrote, and probably my favourite from the first series, the overall plot flows well and I think the introduction of the three new characters is effective, particularly for Andrews's character.

I wanted to have an Australian manager right from the start, however I also wanted to have a manager lose his job, and as the Australian one was the one that needed to stay, he had to be written into episode three rather than being there from the start of series.

This episode also contains my favourite scenes, the spruiker scenes of Andrews, it turns out that spruiker's only exist in Australia, well with that name anyway, they are the people that stand outside a shop and tell you to go in. It took a lot of Google searching to work that out.

BHS Butterfield

Series One – Episode Four

'Over 50's Night'

BHS Butterfield: The Complete First Series

Over 50's Night

Andrew decides that the best way to celebrate his arrival at the hospital is to have a breakfast barbeque for the staff.

In this episode we witness the BHS Butterfield night shift, this night involves going to a call from an Over 50's Nightclub where the staff meet PC Hardy and PC Saxon, very much two characters taken directly from a Black and White movie. The night's events also leave Andrew wondering just what he has to do in order to get rid of some Yorkshire people.

Character List – *in order of appearance*

Dave Parkinson	Yorkshire Man
Joyce Parkinson	Yorkshire Woman
Lizzy Cumming & Eva Knight	Nurses
Biff Wellington	Hospital Chef
Andrew Harris	Australian Manager
Jack Halstead & Chris Lister	Surgeons
Julia Walker	Matron
James Larrey	Paramedic
Molly Hanson	Assistant Manager
Sophie Lizcock	Cleaner
Will Drew	Doctor
Adam Nichols	Mourner
PC Hardy & PC Saxon	Policemen

FADE IN:

1. INT. HOSPITAL WARD - MORNING

We start the day off by visiting the main ward of 'BHS Butterfield' where from the previous day still recovering is Dave and Joyce Parkinson, asleep with bandages in their mouths.

After a few seconds the two hospital nurses, Lizzy Cumming and Eva Knight walk in and take the two bandages out of Dave and Joyce's mouths.

>LIZZY
>Right, get up.

>EVA
>Manager wants a word with the both of you.

They both slowly sit up and look at the two nurses standing in front of them.

>DAVE
>Wha't was t'at?

>LIZZY
>Sorry I can only speak English.

>EVA
>Anyway, the manager wants to see the both of you after breakfast.

>JOYCE
>Oooo and what is for breakfast?

> LIZZY
> Well for us staff, we're having
> a barbecue.

> EVA
> Should be nice.

> JOYCE
> And what about us?

At this moment the hospitals resident chef, Biff Wellington walks into the room and gives the two patients a bowl of 'porridge', that looks like sick.

> DAVE
> Wha't t' is t' this' t'hen

All three of the staff in the room look confused and are unable to understand that Dave has just said.

> JOYCE
> He said, what is this?

> BIFF
> Er... porridge.

> JOYCE
> It looks like sick.

> BIFF
> Yeah, well, we ran out of oats,
> I had to improvise.

2. EXT. OPENING TITLES - DAY

The show's opening titles begin by showing the full front

of the hospital building. As the theme music begins the hospital staff begin to come out of the front door and form as though they are posing for a sports team photo. In the top centre of this formation is the manager. Once the full formation is complete the action freezes and becomes a sketched photo. Over this comes the 'BHS Butterfield' title card.

For the opening titles for episodes three onwards, the original manager is replaced my Andrew.

FADE IN:

3. EXT. BACK GARDEN - MORNING

Into the hospitals back garden where Andrew Harris, the manager of the hospital, is tending to a barbecue, preparing the other staffs bacon sandwiches for breakfast.

Over in the corner are the two hospital surgeons Chris Lister and Jack Halstead, drinking beer. Sat down talking in the other corner is the hospitals matron, Julia Walker and the paramedic, James Larrey.

ANDREW

Grubs up!

At this moment both of the surgeons wave at Andrew, he throws them both a bacon sandwich. They catch them, and then each take a large bite out of them.

Out of the building comes the two nurses, Lizzy and Eva who make sure they walk past the two surgeons on their way to get breakfast.

CHIRS   JACK

Morning Ladies.

Once they have got a sandwich from next to the barbecue they make sure once again they walk past the two surgeons on their way back to the building.

          LIZZY   EVA
Morning Boys.

As they walk back into the house, Biff comes out, he then walks up to the sandwiches and takes 3, before joining Julia and James's conversation.

          BIFF
Morning Andrew.

          ANDREW
Morning mate.

Exiting from the house this time is the hospitals cleaner, Sophie Lizcock who as she walk past, with her cleaning cloth walks up to the two surgeons and wiping ketchup of their chins.

          SOPHIE
You two need bibs.

She then takes a sandwich for herself, walks back over to the surgeons and begins talking to them.

          ANDREW
Anyone seen Molly--

As if by command, at the mention of her name, out of no where, Molly comes running in and jumps on Andrew, they both fall to the floor.

ANDREW (CONT'D)
This morning!

They both now stand up quickly trying to keep what little dignity the have left.

Now making their entrance from the side gate is the hospitals consultant Will Drew and the mourner Adam Nichols.

WILL
Sorry were late.

ADAM
Got, Er, stuck in traffic.

WILL
(to Adam)
Good one!
(to Andrew)
I mean, yeah, got stuck in traffic.

As they begin to walk into the building, Andrew calls to them.

ANDREW
Hold on, don't you both live about 2 minutes away?

They both ignore him but suddenly walk into the house quicker than before.

4.   10 SECOND BREAK UP SHOT #1

4a. INT. MOURNERY/ BATHROOM - DAY

The work day for Adam begins in the hospital mournery located in the bathroom. The room is empty to begin with apart from a body laid in the bath.

Adam walks into the room and sits on the toilet, fully clothed.

He tries talking to the body.

              ADAM
    Morning. I take it you had a
    dead boring night?

5. INT. MANAGERS OFFICE - DAY

We are in the office of Andrew where we find him sat at his desk with his feet up drinking a beer on his own when there is a knock on the door and Molly enters.

            ANDREW
    Do sit down.

Molly follows this request and sits opposite facing Andrew.

             MOLLY
    Isn't it a bit early to be
    drinking?

           ANDREW
    Nope, it is half ten at night.

             MOLLY
    No it isn't

ANDREW
It is in Brisbane.

MOLLY
Well what did you want to see me about?

ANDREW
Well, I've been looking through You're CV, and I think you have a lot of experience and also the quality's to be part of the hospital management.

MOLLY
Really?

ANDREW
Yeah, I think you'd be perfect for it.

Andrew now just sits smiling. This is broken by shouting from outside the room.

DAVE (O.C.)
What does t' bloody criminal wan't from t' us?

CHRIS (O.C.)
Not sure actually.

JACK (O.C.)
Go find out.

DAVE (O.C.)
Aye, I'll give him t' piece of

me.

The office door slams open and Dave is stood there with the two surgeons stood behind him.

> DAVE (CONT'D)
> Righ't' what did you want with t'hee?

> ANDREW
> Still not trying English I see?

> DAVE
> Watch thy blood mouth or thout'll twat thy one.

> MOLLY
> I'll catch up with you later Andrew.

> ANDREW
> Alright, cheers.

Molly leaves the room and her seat is taken by Dave, the two surgeons move to stand behind him, we can see that Chris has his hand hid behind his back.

> DAVE
> What did thy bloody want then?

> ANDREW
> I have your bill for you.

> DAVE
> What d' you mean t' bill?

ANDREW
This is a private hospital, and you have had treatment.

DAVE
How much then?

ANDREW
Er, £400 standard fee, then treatment at £700 and then that injection at £1200.

DAVE
What' injection?

At this point Chris takes his hand out from behind his back to reveal a syringe which he injects into Dave, this makes him fall off his chair.

ANDREW
That one.

CHIRS
Extra strength sedation. It's how Jack gets his women.

ANDREW
Nice. How much are they?

JACK
Err, around £12 I think.

ANDREW
Be fine charging him £1200 then, just the decimal point in the wrong place.

BHS Butterfield: The Complete First Series

>   CHRIS
> What are we doing with him now?

>   ANDREW
> Same injection to his wife, and
> then take them down the road,
> there building a conservatory,
> should be a skip there. I'll
> post the bill.

6.   INT. HOSPITAL STAFF ROOM - MORNING

In the hospitals staff room where Julia and the paramedic James Larrey are sat listening to the radio station. They are both reading a file each, on the front of Julia's there is a sticker that reads 'BHS Butterfield Fatalities, that are officially my fault', whereas on James's there is a sticker that reads, 'Patients that died before reaching BHS Butterfield because I'm too slow'.

>   RADIO PRESENTER (O.S.)
> And now time for the news. We
> can confirm reports of the new
> super flu virus that is
> spreading around the UK rapidly,
> particularly in medical
> environments. This is said to be
> much more dangerous than MRSA.

>   JULIA
> Where are those forensic suits?

>   JAMES
> Why?

>   JULIA

Better to be safe than sorry.

                JAMES
What about the patients?

                JULIA
There already going to die, they don't matter.

7. INT. MANAGERS OFFICE - DAY

Into the office of Andrew again, as usual he is sat with his feet up and a beer in his hand, sat opposite him are the two surgeons, they are also sat with their feet up drinking a beer.

                ANDREW
I've got an idea to save a bit of cash.

                JACK
What is it?

                ANDREW
Prot -- whatever they are limbs and stuff.

                CHRIS
Carry on.

                ANDREW
Well I think we should just make them out of--

Andrew opens the desk draw, he pulls out a whip and places it on the desk.

JACK
A whip?

He goes back to the desk draw and this time pulls out a dildo which he also places onto the table.

CHIRS
And a dildo?

ANDREW
I was looking for blue tack.

CHIRS
I don't think you found it.

ANDREW
These aren't mine.

JACK
Of course.

Once again he goes back into the draw, this third time he pulls out a number of chains.

CHIRS
What exactly are you planning on doing to save some cash?

ANDREW
Whose office was this before I came?

JACK
Would have been Anthony's.

ANDREW

> There his then, I've not cleared this desk out.

Going to the desk again, he pulls out a rubber suit and places that also on the desk.

> CHIRS
> Well I guess at least with the suit there won't be room to move so they'll be no need for the prosthetic limbs.

> JACK
> Hold on, what's that on the side?

Jacks picks up the dildo and points out an inscription on the side which Chris reads out.

> CHRIS
> Julia's?

Jack suddenly drops it, Andrew then picks it up to take a closer look at it, as he does, Molly walks into the room carrying a mug.

Andrew panics and suddenly drops it before quickly clearing the desk with one swipe of his hand, knocking it all on the floor.

> MOLLY
> What was all that?

> ANDREW
> Nothing.

MOLLY
I brought you a coffee.

She places the coffee on the table. Before leaving the room.

ANDREW
Thank-you.
    (to the surgeons)
Makes up for the beer.

JACK
Why didn't you just tell her what they were?

CHIRS
Yeah, maybe she'd let you use them on her?

ANDREW
Are you two always this dirty?

JACK
Are you saying you wouldn't give her one?

Julia now walks into the room and picks up the stuff on the floor.

JULIA
I've been looking for this, lent it to Anthony a while back.
    (to the Surgeons)
By the way, Molly is stood just outside the door and can hear everything your saying.

THAT NIGHT

8. INT. HOSPITAL STAFF ROOM - NIGHT

We are in the hospitals staff room, late at night, where sat on one of the sofas is Chris Lister, laid half asleep, with a balloon in his mouth which he keeps blowing up and letting back down again.

After doing this a few times, Jack appears from behind the back of the sofa, just as the balloon becomes fully blown up, Jack claps on it and pops it, startling Chris and making him fully alert.

                CHIRS
What the fuck are you doing?

                JACK
Being a good mate?

                CHRIS
And how exactly is nearly giving me a heart attack and killing me being a good mate?

Chris now gets another balloon and begins to blow that one up as well.

                JACK
I never said being a good mate to you. Just to society, and look on the upside you are in a hospital.

Chris who is now holding the fully blown up balloon lets

go of it, the balloon fly's around the room.

>   CHRIS
> I always do appreciate your sarcasm at 1 in the morning.

>   JACK
> Don't worry, I wasn't being sarcastic. What are you doing with balloons anyway?

>   CHRIS
> Just bored. These night shifts are shit.

>   JACK
> I thought you were just practicing for your next woman, they always take a bit of blowing up.

9. INT. HALLWAY - NIGHT - CONTINUOUS

We not go to the main hallway of the BHS Butterfield building.

The hallway is empty until out of one of the side rooms comes the hospitals paramedic James Larrey.

>   JAMES
>   (shouting)
> Listen up! Call out, party, not sure of the details, we need all the people we can get.

>   CHRIS (O.C.)

We're awake.

                    JACK (O.C.)
For once.

                    BIFF (O.C.)
I'll get the sandwiches.

                    MOLLY (O.C.)
Make that coffee.

                    WILL (O.C.)
With a dash of vodka.

                    JULIA (O.C.)
I'll fetch the bandages.

                    ANDREW (O.C.)
Has anyone ever told you that
bandages are not the solution to
every single fucking problem.

There is a pause, then.

                    WILL (O.C.)
Can we add a dash of vodka to
that as well?

10. 10 SECOND BREAK UP SHOT #2

11. EXT. OUTSIDE HOUSE - NIGHT

We now go to the outside of a house where there has been a party.

There is police tape cordoning off the house, stood

outside the front door are two police officers, PC Saxon and PC Hardy.

From down the street, running, comes the staff of BHS Butterfield, leading at the front is Andrew, behind him is Will, Jack, Chris, Julia, James, Biff and Molly.

They get to the door of the house. As they do both police officers bend down.

      PC SAXON
Ello ello ello.

      PC HARDY
And who are you lot?

      ANDREW
An Aussie.
   (pointing at the
   surgeons)
The chuckle brothers.
   (pointing at Will)
Doctor who.
   (pointing at Biff)
Jamie Oliver.
   (pointing at James)
James May the ambulance driver.
   (pointing at Julia and
   Molly)
And some woman.

      PC SAXON
Oh, hello, me and PC Hardy have a bit of a thing for woman.

      PC HARDY

Yes, that is very true PC Saxon, I've never seen one up close before.

MOLLY
I cannot imagine why.

ANDREW
Don't worry, in the case of Julia, you're not missing out.

PC SAXON
Well sir, Are you here for the party?

ANDREW
Well, what's left of it.

PC HARDY
Ah well sir, I should probably tell you what's been going on.

JACK
We'll all go in and see what we can do.

PC SAXON
Very good sir. We'll tell this young sir what's happened.

All of the other staff go inside of the house and leave Andrew stood with the two police officers.

PC HARDY
Well you see sir, this house here was being used for an over

50's night.

ANDREW
What do you mean over 50's night.

PC SAXON
Well sir, there a group of people that every month meet up and create an over 50's night club at one of the groups house.

ANDREW
Right.

PC HARDY
They've all had a bit too much of the old alcohol sir, and things got a bit out of hand.

PC SAXON
We did dismiss the majority and they went home, but you see sir, there are still a few that remain that need a bit of your medical treatment sir.

ANDREW
Okay, I'll see what I can do.

PC HARDY
That's very good sir.

12. INT. LIVING ROOM - NIGHT

We go to the living room of the house now, where Chris,

BHS Butterfield: The Complete First Series

Jack and Will are sat around not doing their jobs.

Andrew walks into the room, he looks confused.

          ANDREW
Why aren't any of you doing any work?

          CHIRS
We never do any work.

          JACK
James is upstairs with some woman who won't stop being sick, Molly and Julia are sorting the fight out that happened in the garden.

          ANDREW
Where's Biff? Why did we bring a chef anyway?

          CHIRS
Getting the tea's in, he always comes on these trips, its cheaper than shopping is.

          WILL
I did find two people in the garage, but, I don't think we should treat them.

          ANDREW
Why?

          WILL

Go look yourself.

Looking confused, Andrew walks out of the room.

> CHIRS
> (to Jack)
> Spoons?

> JACK
> What? I'm not spooning here.

> CHIRS
> No, spoons.

> JACK
> Oh, yeah, go get some.

Will now looks confused, Chris gets up and exits the room.

13. INT. HOUSE KITCHEN - CONTINUOUS

Now to the kitchen of the house which they are at where we find Biff running around the room trying to make tea, when Chris walks into the room.

> CHIRS
> Do you have any spoons?

> BIFF
> Yeah, I think there's some in
> that draw.

Biff walks over to one of the draws and opens it, Chris takes out 3 wooden spoons before leaving the room.

Taking a bag out of his pocket, Biff begins to then empty

the contents of the draw into the bag.

>   BIFF (CONT'D)
>   (to himself)
>   Could do with some new cutlery.

14.   EXT. BACK GARDEN - NIGHT

Into the back garden of the house, we see Molly and Julia holding back two old woman from fighting with each other.

>   OLD WOMAN 1
>   You bitch, I'm going to slap you
>   to death.

>   OLD WOMAN 2
>   You're a complete hag.

>   MOLLY
>   (to Julia)
>   Shouldn't this be the police's
>   job?

>   JULIA
>   (to Molly)
>   Probably yes.

>   OLD WOMAN 1
>   You slept with my Harold you
>   slag.

>   MOLLY
>   (to Julia)
>   I think I've found the perfect
>   matches for Chris and Jack.

15.   INT. BATHROOM - NIGHT

A visit to the bathroom now, where we find James lent over an old woman who keeps throwing up in the toilet.

> JAMES
> That's it, just be sick as much as you need to be.

The woman stops being sick after a few seconds, she then looks up at James, this makes her be sick again.

16.   INT. LIVING ROOM - NIGHT - CONTINUOUS

We go to the living room of the house where we re-join the action with Chris, Jack and Will.

Sat on the sofa in the middle is Will with Chris sat next to him and Jack sat on the arm at the other side drinking.

All three of them have a wooden spoon, however Jack is hiding his away from Will.

> CHRIS
> You never tried this before?

> WILL
> Not that I can remember. Maybe when I was pissed.

> JACK
> Plenty of opportunities there.

> WILL
> Fuck off.

CHRIS
Right, here's what we do. Put it in your mouth like this.
(he puts the spoon into his mouth)
Then you put your head down.

Will bows his head towards Chris.

CHRIS (CONT'D)
Then.

Chris moves the spoon down and hits Will with it on top of the head.

WILL
That's it?

CHRIS
Yep, see who his hardest.

Will places the spoon in his mouth and hits Chris in the same way.

JACK
That's pathetic mate.

CHRIS
Go again.

Will does the same.

CHRIS (CONT'D)
Fucking hell! I thought you might be half decent at this.

                    WILL
Well show me how it's done then.

                    CHRIS
Alright, I will.

Will bows his head again. Chris hits it again but as he does this time Jack whacks his head with the spoon he has.

                    WILL
Ah fuck man!

                    JACK
What's up?

                    WILL
That--

                    JACK
He's good at it.

                    WILL
How do you do that...?

                    CHRIS
I'll show you.

Will bows his head once again and as last time when Chris goes to hit him, Jack whacks him.

                    WILL
              (rubbing his head)
Shit twat fucking bitch.

                    CHRIS
Jack's mum isn't here.

Will looks up at Chris still rubbing his head as he does.

                WILL
One more time--

As before, when Chris goes to hit him Jack instead whacks him. Will now rubs his head even more.

                JACK
I think it might all be in the neck movement.

Andrew now walks back into the room looking annoyed.

                WILL
I take it you've looked in the garage.

                ANDREW
Yes I have.
        (to the Surgeons)
I thought I told you both to make sure they went into a skip?

                CHIRS
Who's this?

Behind Andrew now appears Dave Parkinson, the Yorkshire man.

                DAVE
Righ't then t' lad.

                JACK
Oh.

                    DAVE
          I wan't t' word with you t'.

                    ANDREW
          Can I borrow a spoon?

Chris hands Andrew one of the spoons. Andrew then turns and drags Dave out of the room.

There is a small pause before we hear the crack of wood on Skin.

Andrew re appears rubbing his head, he was the one who was hit.

                    ANDREW (CONT'D)
          Might need another spoon.

Jack and Will hand there spoons over to Andrew before he leaves the room again.

What now follows is the sound of wood on skin, many times.

                    CHIRS
          Anyone up for just going home?

                    JACK
          Yeah.

All three of them leave the room.

17. EXT. BACK GARDEN - NIGHT

Back to the action in the back garden where Molly and Julia are still separating the two old women from fighting.

The old women keep shouting insults at each other throughout the scene.

> MOLLY
> I don't really think we should keep standing here.

> JULIA
> I agree, this isn't really out job.

> MOLLY
> Let's just go.

At the same time Molly and Julia let go of the two women who immediately both start fighting with each other.

Molly and Julia walk off.

18. INT. OUTSIDE HOUSE- NIGHT

Again at the outside of the house, where PC Saxon and PC Hardy are still standing.

All of the staff come out of the front door apart from Andrew.

> PC HARDY
> Are you all leaving already?

> PC SAXON
> That is a good observation PC Hardy. Don't you have some people to treat in there?

> MOLLY

Did it all.

> PC HARDY
> Really? That's good service.

> JACK
> We pride ourselves on it.

> CHIRS
> Anyone seen Andrew?

Andrew now appears from the house rubbing his head and holding a spoon.

> JACK
> Who won?

> ANDREW
> Head hurts, a lot.

> CHIRS
> (in a patronizing tone)
> Aww, did little Andrew get beaten up by the big bad Yorkshire man.

Molly walks up to Andrew and gives him a kiss on the head.

> PC HARDY
> Oh, PC Saxon, Looks like there's something going on here.

> PC SAXON
> Yes it does PC Hardy, The starting's of something there.

> JACK
> Aww, did Molly kiss little Andrew better?

Andrew walks up to jack, spoon in hand.

> FADE TO BLACK:

There is now another loud crack.

THE NEXT MORNING

19. INT. HOSPITAL STAFF ROOM - DAY

It is now the next morning and we are in the staff room of the hospital where Andrew, Chris and Jack are sat on the sofas talking.

> CHIRS
> Rough night.

> ANDREW
> Whose stupid idea is an over 50's night club anyway?

> JACK
> Someone over 50 at a guess.

> ANDREW
> And what is it with that Yorkshire couple, they never go away.

Molly now enters the room and sits next to Andrew, as she does this Jack gets his phone out and starts playing the song 'Puppy Love'. Andrew just stares at him.

                    ANDREW (CONT'D)
        Fuck off!

20.   CLOSING TITLES

21.   INT. SPARE ROOM - DAY

    We are in the hospital spare room looking down at the floor where we can see a number of different items of clothing.

    Chris walks into the room and notices the items on the floor, he pushes some aside to find the items Andrew found in his desk earlier under them, all apart from the dildo.

    Chris looks up towards the bed however we cannot see what he is looking at, he simply stares.

                    JULIA (O.C.)
        Oh, Hello Chris. Care to join
        me?

    Chris faints and falls on the floor.

    THE END

BHS Butterfield: The Complete First Series

Note from the Writer

Episode four has a bit of everything, spooning, sort of, some bitch old women, old fashioned police, a barbeque and the start of a love story.

I am in no way responsible for any injury that you or anyone else occur from using scene 16 in real life, but feel free to set a friend up with that one, I am not responsible if they punch you in the face though.

This episode has quite a noticeable split to it, the first half is very much focused on the hospital staff whereas the second is set in the over 50's nightclub. Initially, this was going to be the episode Angus was to write however when he found out that he can't write, I had to quickly come up with an idea and do it myself.

BHS Butterfield: The Complete First Series

BHS Butterfield

Series One – Episode Five

'Aussie v Kiwi'

BHS Butterfield: The Complete First Series

Aussie v Kiwi

The series one finale episode. In this episode we meet the character of Huihana Ngaruruku, the cousin of Andrew from New Zealand. In the previous two episodes, there were a lot of jokes made about Aussies and so in this episode it was time to sort that out.

This episode has plenty of jokes between the characters and leaves many cliff-hangers for series two. Enjoy the series one finale.

Character List – *in order of appearance*

Huihana Ngaruruku	Andrews Cousin
Andrew Harris	Australian Manager
Will Drew	Doctor
Jack Halstead & Chris Lister	Surgeons
Molly Hanson	Assistant Manager
Biff Wellington	Hospital Chef
Julia Walker	Matron
Zoe Lynch	Doctor
James Larrey	Paramedic
Adam Nichols	Mourner
Lizzy Cumming & Eva Knight	Nurses

BHS Butterfield: The Complete First Series

FADE IN:

1. INT. HALLWAY - MORNING

We begin in the main hallway of the house in the morning, the hallway is empty.

After a few seconds we can see someone appear at the front door followed by a knock, then another knock.

Out of a door comes the hospitals Australian Manager, Andrew Harris, he walks up and opens the front door.

As the door opens we can see Andrews New Zealand cousin, Huihana Ngaruruku, standing there, she smiles at Andrew.

                HUIHANA
          (sub. Hello)
Kia ora bro!

                ANDREW
Fuck off!

                HUIHANA
          (sub. Sorry?)
Aroha mai?

                ANDREW
I meant come in.

                HUIHANA
          (sub. Thank you so very
          much)
Tena rawa atu koe!

At this Huihana walks in, leaving Andrew standing stood

looking shocked. She dumps her luggage in the hallway before continuing through to the staff room.

2. INT. HOSPITAL STAFF ROOM - MORNING - CONTINUOUS

Sitting on the sofas is the two hospital surgeons, Chris Lister and Jack Halstead and asleep on the floor is the consultant doctor Will Drew.

The door opens and Huihana walks in followed by Andrew who still looks shocked.

                HUIHANA
         (sub. Hello There)
Kia ora ara!

                CHRIS
Hi.

                JACK
         (winks)
Hello.

                ANDREW
This is my cousin.

Chris throws a pillow at Will to wake him up.

                CHRIS
Hey will, we have company.

Will sits up and looks at Huihana.

                WILL
Wow.

3. EXT. OPENING TITLES - DAY

The show's opening titles begin by showing the full front of the hospital building. As the theme music begins the hospital staff begin to come out of the front door and form as though they are posing for a sports team photo. In the top centre of this formation is the manager. Once the full formation is complete the action freezes and becomes a sketched photo. Over this comes the 'BHS Butterfield' title card.

For the opening titles for episodes three onwards, the original manager is replaced my Andrew.

4. INT. HOSPITAL STAFF ROOM - MORNING

We carry off from where the scene was before the opening titles.

> ANDREW
> Well, I'll leave you all to talk,
> I've got to go check on a patient.

Andrew now walks out of the room.

5. INT. HALLWAY - MORNING - CONTINUOUS

We are now out in the hallway again as Andrew comes out of the staff room. He turns faces the wall and head-butts it.

At this moment the assistant hospital manager Molly Hanson walks down the stair and comes to stand next to Andrew.

> MOLLY
> What's wrong?

ANDREW
My cousins here.

MOLLY
Is that not a good thing?

ANDREW
She's from New Zealand.

MOLLY
Ah.

Andrew now looks up and faces molly.

ANDREW
Right, well I'm sure there's something I can be pretending to do around here.

MOLLY
I think I'll join you.

6. INT. HOSPITAL WARD - MOMENTS LATER

Now we take our first visit of the day to the hospitals ward. Lying on the floor is Patient One. Preparing a concoction of medicine in the corner of the room is the hospital Matron Julia Walker.

Andrew enters the room along with Molly. The go and look over the patient who is sat up.

ANDREW
G'day there.

PATIENT ONE

Good morning.

>MOLLY
>May we ask what's wrong with you?

Julia walks over and hands the patient the concoction which she was preparing.

>PATIENT ONE
>I'm not sure exactly, I've been told a blockage of some sort.

The patient takes a sip of the drink, then falls still.

>MOLLY
>Were you given any more information?

There is no reply. After a few seconds.

>ANDREW
>Err, Julia, what was in that?

>JULIA
>Bleach.

>ANDREW
>Why?

>JULIA
>Well it worked unblocking the toilets the other day.

>MOLLY
>I'll go get Adam.

7. EXT. CONSULTING AREA - MORNING

We go now to the outdoor consulting area where a patio table set is out.

Sitting at one side of the table is Patient One, Leah Firth, facing, sat on the other side is Zoe Lynch, a doctor of the hospital, she looks professional.

>   ZOE
> Good morning Miss Firth.
>
>   LEAH
> Good morning.
>
>   ZOE
> May I ask your symptoms?
>
>   LEAH
> Well I've just been feeling more and more ill the past week.
>
>   ZOE
> Where about is this illness been centred?
>
>   LEAH
> Around the stomach area.
>
>   ZOE
> Well It doesn't sound too serious. I'm going to prescribe you with some antibiotics.

Suddenly out of nowhere comes a rugby ball that hits Zoe in the side of the face.

The camera zooms out to reveal Chris, Jack and Will along with Huihana. It is not clear who has thrown it.

Zoe turns to them.

> ZOE (CONT'D)
> (angry)
> What do you think you are doing.
> This is a hospital.

From an open window.

> ANDREW
> Good shot.

They all look up at the window to see Andrew and Molly looking out of it.

> HUIHANA
> Coming to join us cuz?

> ANDREW
> I wouldn't say no.

Andrew and Molly now disappear from the window and the action returns to Zoe and her Patient Leah.

> ZOE
> As I was saying, this is a hospital. I am trying to care for my patients, I know that is not Something that any of you do but--

> LEAH
> (to huihana)
> Mind if I join you.

> HUIHANA
> That'll be choice!

Out of the back door behind them come Andrew and Molly, Andrew picks up the ball that is behind Zoe.

> ZOE
> Is there any staff here who take their responsibility even the slightest bit seriously?

Zoe turns round and faces Andrew, just as he throws the ball to her head.

> ANDREW
> Sorry.

Zoe slaps him before storming off.

> WILL
> That looked painful.

> HUIHANA
> Not the first time he's been slapped and won't be the last.

> ANDREW
> How is your mum?

> HUIHANA
> Much better now she's got rid of the smell.

> ANDREW
> How's your dad about it?

HUIHANA
He can't quite get rid of it still.

CHRIS
Sorry what's this?

JACK
Yeah, I also have that question.

HUIHANA
Last November, back in --

ANDREW
OK that's enough of that.

8. 10 SECOND BREAK UP SHOT #1

9. INT. HOSPITAL STAFF ROOM - MORNING

Back to the hospitals staff room now where sat on one of the sofas is Zoe talking to the hospital paramedic James Larrey who is sat on the other.

ZOE
What is it with this place?

JAMES
What do you mean?

ZOE
All of the staff.

JAMES
Still not getting you?

ZOE

No one seems to actually do there job.

                JAMES
Well I do, I'm always putting my job first.

The door to the staff room opens. Molly enters.

                MOLLY
Hey James, we need a ref.

                JAMES
I'm coming.

Molly leaves the room again with James following behind.

                ZOE
            (to herself)
This is too fucking far now.

10.   EXT. CONSULTING AREA - MORNING

Back now to the hospital consulting area where Huihana, Andrew, Chris, Jack, Will and Jordan are talking.

Walking out of the house comes Molly followed by James who both join the action. As they do this, Andrew who currently has the ball throws it to Molly, they all begin to pass it between each other while talking.

                HUIHANA
            (to Andrew)
Don't you have patients to be looking after?

ANDREW
Yep.

HUIHANA
And are you planning on, you know, doing the looking after?

ANDREW
Nope.

HUIHANA
Choice!

ANDREW
Yep.

CHRIS
So you two are cousins then?

At this point the ball is thrown to Jack however he doesn't catch it and the ball rolls away. He goes to fetch it.

HUIHANA
Yeah.

JACK
So are you both Aussie then?

Jack picks up the ball just as Huihana takes a run up and rugby tackles him to the ground.

As he is tacked the ball fly's into the air and is caught by Andrew.

ANDREW
Bit of advice mate, never call a

Kiwi an Aussie. Especially her.

                    JACK

Ow.

Out of the house comes Julia running.

                    JULIA

I have bandages.

11. INT. HOSPITAL WARD - MORNING

Back to the hospitals ward now where the patient from earlier is laid dead in the same position.

Standing over the patient is the hospitals two nurses Eva Knight and Lizzy Cumming. Adam Nichols the hospitals mourner now enters the room.

                    ADAM

This the one?

                    LIZZY

Yep.

                    ADAM

What happened?

                    EVA

Julia.

                    ADAM

As usual, something to do with bandages by any chance?

                    LIZZY

No, bleach this time.

                ADAM
That's new, anyway, let's get this body out of here.

Adam takes the arms of the patient and begins to drag them out of the room, just a Zoe walks in.

                ZOE
I wasn't expecting that!

                ADAM
Expecting what?

                ZOE
You to be the only one working.

                ADAM
What do you mean only one?

                ZOE
All the rest are off playing rugby.

At this point Adam drops the patient and walks out of the room.

                ZOE (CONT'D)
Fucking typical.
       (to the nurses)
You staying to help?

                EVA
Well--

                LIZZY

No.

12. EXT. PARK - DAY

The action now fades to a large open park. The shot starts wide and we are able to see the staff of BHS Butterfield warming up and preparing themselves for the match ahead.

The staff are separated into two separate groups preparing at either side of the field. On one side is Andrews team made up of himself, Molly, Leah, Biff and Sophie.

Facing them on the other side is Huihana's team made up of herself, Will, Chris, Jack, Lizzy and Eva.

Stood on the side-lines is Adam with a megaphone and Julia with a box of bandages. James is stood in the middle of the field with a whistle to ref the match.

                    ADAM
            (in style of commentator)
      Welcome to this match between New
      Zealand and Australia, the teams
      are much different from the usual,
      and so is the pitch for that
      matter. Moving on.

The scene is now focused on Huihana and the rest of her team are stood facing Andrew and his.

[DIALOUGE HERE HAS BEEN OMMITED FOR CULTURAL AND INTELECTUAL PROERTY REASONS]

                    ADAM
            (in style of commentator)
      And so there it is, the challenge

has been set by this unusual New
Zealand team. However Australia has
something to say about this.

The scene now focuses on Andrew and his team who are huddled together as though they are having a team chat.

They instead however begin to do the Hokey Cokey.

> ANDREW'S TEAM
> You put your right leg in, your right leg out, In, Out, In, Out, You shake it all about, You do the hokey cokey and you turn around, that's what it's all about. Whoa, the hokey cokey! Whoa, the hokey cokey, Whoa, the hokey cokey, knees bent, arms stretched, Rah! Rah! Rah!

Andrew turns round and faces Huihana.

> ANDREW
> (sub. Fuck you)
> Hamuti!

> ADAM
> And there it is, Australia's answer, Showing that they will not be intimidated by this New Zealand side.

The two teams are now facing each other ready to start the match. James blows his whistle and Huihana's team kicks off.

> ADAM (CONT'D)
> And they're off!

3 MINUTES IMPROVISED PLAYING

VOICE OVER THIS: ADAMS COMMENTRY OF THE MATCH

After a few minutes the action cuts to Andrew having the ball, running towards the try line with Huihana in his way.

When he gets within a few meters of her he suddenly stops, turns and runs back towards his own team. Huihana runs after him and tackles him to the ground hard.

Julia comes running onto the field with her box of bandages.

    JULIA
I'm coming!

    ANDREW
Please... Just Don't!

    BIFF
Ooo, this could be a sticky situation.

13. 10 SECOND BREAK UP SHOT #2

14. EXT. BACK GARDEN - AFTERNOON

We are now in the back garden to the hospital building where Huihana is sat on the grass with the two surgeons.

    HUIHANA
Don't you have any work or something to do?

    CHRIS
Yeah but--

JACK
We can't be bothered.

HUIHANA
Chur!

Andrew walks out of the building along with Molly. His arm is in a sling.

HUIHANA (CONT'D)
Broken?

ANDREW
Na, just sprained.

HUIHANA
Well it'll certainly stop a repeat of last time.

CHRIS
Last time?

HUIHANA
Yeah, he nearly fingered a kangaroo.

JACK
Not a wallaby then?

HUIHANA
Na, that would have been illegal, under age and all that.

CHRIS
Hasn't stopped him before.

ANDREW
Can I just point out, It was a bet and I was drunk.

MOLLY
So what happened in the end?

ANDREW
Our other cousin fingered it instead.

HUIHANA
Yeah then Andrew had a fight with it.

ANDREW
Anyway, you up for a babie?

HUIHANA
Yea, keen as bro. But I'm doing the cooking, nearly died when you cooked last.

ANDREW
Yeah but to be fair, that wasn't from my cooking.

HUIHANA
That's true, although I still don't understand how you managed to set both of us on fire... by accident.

ANDREW
I've told you before, Hamilton makes me aggressive.

                        HUIHANA
        We were in Invercargill.

                        ANDREW
        Ah yes, the lovely New Zealand
        Southland, population
        100,000, yet only--

                        HUIHANA
        You don't need to finish that.

15. INT. HOSPITAL WARD - AFTERNOON - CONTINUOUS

We now go back to the hospital ward, where the patient from earlier in the morning is still laid in the same place on the floor.

In the corner of the room is Zoe treating another patient.

Julia enters the room, stepping over the patient on the floor and walking over to Zoe.

                        JULIA
        So, are you coming out for the BBQ?

                        ZOE
        No I certainly am not, I have
        patients to look after.

                        JULIA
        Come on, Have a break.

                        ZOE
        Staying in here is more of a break
        then being with those idiots.

JULIA
There not that bad.

ANDREW (O.S.)
(from outside)
Ahh, Fuck!

HUIHANA (O.S.)
(from outside)
Don t bring that near me!

ANDREW (O.S.)
(from outside)
I don't plan to, you're not fucking touching anything.

BIFF (O.S.)
(from outside)
Calm down, just stick it in there.

ANDREW (O.S.)
(from outside)
Great, now it's wet!

ZOE
You were saying.

JULIA
OK, well there not all idiot's, take Adam for example.

At that moment Adam walks into the room.

ADAM
So who's the dead one?

He walks further into the room and trips over the body on the floor.

> ZOE
> I have honestly had fucking enough of this.

Zoe stands up and storms out of the room. Before re entering a few seconds later.

> ZOE (CONT'D)
> Tell Andrew, I'll meet him in his office.

> ANDREW (O.S.)
> (from outside)
> That smells horrible.

> BIFF (CONT'D)
> (from outside)
> To be fair, you shouldn't be doing that with a fish anyway.

Zoe disappears from view again.

16. EXT. BACK GARDEN - CONTINUOUS

Now back out to the garden where two barbecues are set up. Sat around is the two surgeons, Huihana, Molly and Biff who is holding a fish.

Andrew is sat with his hand in a bucket of water.

Julia walks out of the building.

> JULIA

I don't want to know.

> BIFF
> It involved a fish.

> JULIA
> I know. Oh and Andrew, Zoe would like to see you in your office.

> ANDREW
> What the fuck about?

> JULIA
> She said she's had enough.

> ANDREW
> Fine.

Andrew gets up and walks back into the building.

17. INT. HOSPITAL WARD - AFTERNOON

Back to the hospital ward again where the two patients are still as they were, and Adam is still on the floor after tripping over one of them.

> ADAM
> (to himself)
> I'm sure there's a reason why I'm here.

18. 10 SECOND BREAK UP SHOT #3

19. INT. MANAGERS OFFICE - AFTERNOON

Now to the manager's office, set out as usual with a number

of Australian articles.

Already sat in the room is Zoe, still looking annoyed, the door swings open and Andrew enters throwing himself onto his chair and putting his feet up on the desk.

          ANDREW
Go on then.

Throughout this 'speech' Andrew looks increasingly bored.

          ZOE
Well, I want to say how much of a disgrace this place is, no one at all takes their job even the slightest bit seriously, there is no work standards what so ever, I don't think people here have ever heard the meaning of the word Health and Safety.

          ANDREW
That'll be because Health and Safety is actually three words.

          ZOE
All anyone ever does is joke about, it's ridiculous.

          ANDREW
What's wrong with a bit of humour in the workplace.

          ZOE
Everything, this is a hospital.

ANDREW
No, this is my hospital. And we need people to joke about, gives the patients morale, and makes up for just how serious you are.

ZOE
Well I am serious about this. I wish to resign.

ANDREW
Really?

ZOE
Yes, I never joke about.

ANDREW
In which case I just need to make a quick phone call to Biff.

Andrew pulls his phone out of his pocket and dials Biffs number. After a few seconds of ringing.

BIFF (O.S.)
Mate.

ANDREW
How much meats on the babie?

BIFF (O.S.)
Quite a bit.

ANDREW
Tell Chris and Jack to go down to the shops, and get a bit more, along with a lot of alcohol.

                    BIFF (O.S.)
          Why? What's going on.

                    ANDREW
          Zoe's resigned.

                    BIFF (O.S.)
          How much alcohol?

                    ANDREW
          As much as you want it's on me.

Andrew hangs up on the phone, places it back in his pocket, before sitting up straight and putting a serious look on his face. He takes a deep breath.

                    ANDREW (CONT'D)
          So Zoe, would you like help
          packing?

20.   INT. HOSPITAL WARD - AFTERNOON

The hospital ward where Adam is still laid on the floor not bothering to move with the two dead patients laid next to him. He attempts to make conversation with them.

                    ADAM
          So, have you ever thought about how
          you'd like to die?

There is no response from either of the patients. Andrew appears behind Adam at the door but doesn't say anything, Adam does not notice he's there.

                    ADAM (CONT'D)
          Personally, I'd like to go like my

Granddad did, in my sleep... unlike
the passengers screaming and
shouting in his car.

          ANDREW
      (imitating one of the
      patients)
My dad died in a car crash.

At this Adam has a brief period of shock, before he turns
over to look at Andrew standing above him.

          ADAM
I think I've just had a heart
attack.

          ANDREW
Well I have told you to eat less.

          ADAM
What do you want?

          ANDREW
Came to tell you that you don't
need to depose of those bodies.

          ADAM
Why?

          ANDREW
We'll barbecue them, were running
out of coal, having a celebration.

          ADAM
In aid of.

> ANDREW
> Zoe's resignation.

> ADAM
> Fuck yes.

> ANDREW
> Yeah, don't do that to them.

LATER THAT DAY

21. INT. HOSPITAL STAFF ROOM - EVENING

Sat around the room is the two surgeons, Biff, James and Adam. All are half asleep.

Zoe walks into the room. No one pays attention to her.

> ZOE
> Well I've just handed in my notice, and I know we've not really--

> ADAM
> (turning to the surgeons)
> You two want to take care of this?

> ZOE
> Had a good --

> JACK
> Na, we kicked Anthony out.

> CHRIS
> You can have the pleasure this time.

ZOE
Working relationship--

BIFF
I'll help you.

ZOE
But I—

ADAM
Let's do it.

ZOE
Just want.

Mid speech Adam and Biff stand up and push Zoe out of the room, a few seconds later we hear the door slam.

JAMES
(as though he doesn't
know what just happened)
What was that?

CHRIS
Nothing important.

Andrew now walks into the room holding a beer.

ANDREW
Right, she's gone, we have food and alcohol.

Molly walks into the room and gives Andrew a hug.

MOLLY
You can eat me if you want Aussie

boy.

                ANDREW
How much have you been drinking?

22.   EXT. BACK GARDEN - NIGHT

We are in the back garden of the hospital where there is a party in full swing, with all the hospital staff, Huihana and a lot of the patients.

We are focused on Chris, Jack and Biff who are stood watching Andrew and Molly laughing with each other.

                CHRIS
If they weren't both drunk, it would be kind of cute.

                BIFF
Molly's not actually drunk a thing all night.

                JACK
What? You mean she's actually interested in him?

                BIFF
There interested in each other, they just won't tell each other.

                CHRIS
How do you know?

                BIFF
They told me.

The two hospital nurses, Lizzy Cumming and Eva Knight walk up to the two surgeons and grab them by the hand dragging them off.

>LIZZY
>Come with us boys.

>EVA
>We want to talk to you.

>BIFF
>See you later guys.

Biff turns round to find Julia in his face, she starts to hug him.

>BIFF
>Is this what a bit of alcohol does to everyone? -- Hold on, aren't you married?

23. INT. CLOSING TITLES

THE NEXT MORNING

24. EXT. OUTSIDE FRONT OF BUILDING - MORNING

To the outside of the hospital building in the evening now.

Stood there talking is Andrew and Huihana.

>ANDREW
>Right, well better give you a lift back to the airport.

>HUIHANA

Alright cuz. I appreciate it.

              ANDREW
You're welcome to come visit any time.

              HUIHANA
As are you. If you're allowed back in NZ yet.

              ANDREW
Couple more years.

The two of them now hug in a friendly way and arm round each other they walk off. We are able to see a sign pointing downwards on the back of Andrew, the sign reads 'To the Outback'.

              JACK
I know she's a kiwi, but she's got a good sense of humour.

The camera now zooms back to show the two surgeons standing watching.

              CHRIS
Aww, isn't family love so good to see.

              JACK
You're not wrong there.

They now turn to each other, and hug emotionally.

              CHRIS
I love you brother.

> JACK
> I love you to.

> FADE TO BLACK.

> JACK (CONT'D)
> Hold on, is there something your not telling me? I didn't know we were brothers.

THE END

BHS Butterfield: The Complete First Series

Note from the Writer

Readers who are not Aussie or Kiwi will most likely be sat wondering what quite a few of the references they have just read actually are. I wanted BHS Butterfield to have a wide international audience and so an episode full of Australian and New Zealand references was required.

Introduced in this episode is Huihana Ngaruruku, this name is of course not in English, it's Maori, Huihana translates into English as Lily.

Being an All Blacks supporter I found it quite hard to use them and New Zealand as a target for jokes in this episode. Having previously met a number of the Maori All Blacks, notably Andre Taylor, Jamison Gibson Park and Jarred Hoeata, while I can comment on how friendly they all are, they are not the sort of people I would particularly like to take the piss out of too their face.

This episode has been written in a way that leaves series two with plots that could go one of many ways.

BHS Butterfield: The Complete First Series

BHS Butterfield

Series Two – Episode Three

'A Day for Love'

BHS Butterfield: The Complete First Series

A Day for Love

The only episode that was written for series two (so far anyway), I think this is one of the best episodes and so I decided to include it in this book.

In this episode we see Andrew and Molly finally getting together and joining Jack as he goes out for a meal date with his less than perfect girlfriend Louise. Not wanting their friend to miss out, Andrew and Jack make sure that Chris also has a woman for the evening.

Character List – *in order of appearance*

Jack Halstead & Chris Lister	Surgeons
Andrew Harris	Australian Manager
Biff Wellington	Hospital Chef
Molly Hanson	Assistant Manager
Julia Walker	Matron
Miss Nichols	Old Woman
Louise	Jacks Girlfriend
Anthony Young	Original Manager
Adam Nichols	Mourner

BHS Butterfield: The Complete First Series

FADE IN:

1. INT. DARK HALLWAY - EARLY MORNING

We are in a dark hallway for BHS Butterfield early in the morning. We cannot see anything apart from a dim light coming from a slightly open door at the end of the hallway.

              WOMAN (O.C.)
Well come on then get hard.

              CHRIS (O.C.)
That is hard.

              WOMAN (O.C.)
Is that the best you can do?

              CHRIS (O.C.)
I'm paying you stop taking the fucking piss.

              WOMAN (O.C.)
You need to pay extra for that size, tastes worse.

              CHRIS (O.C.)
Fuck you then fuck off.

              WOMAN (O.C.)
I thought that was what I was here for.

              CHRIS (O.C.)
Get out. Fuck you, expensive as fuck.

> WOMAN (O.C.)
> I think you mean expensive to fuck.

We can hear movement from the room before the door opens and Chris walks out pushing the woman out. Both are half naked. She walks off.

Chris stands there staring at the camera as the next door opens and Andrew, the Australian Manager walks out and stands behind him without him noticing.

> ANDREW
> Morning.

> CHRIS
> (startled)
> Fucking hell mate.

> ANDREW
> Really, didn't sound like you got much of that.

> CHRIS
> (walking back into the room)
> Fuck off mate!

> ANDREW
> Hey don't be like that. What do you do with a years' worth of used condoms?

> JACK (O.C.)
> Melt them down, makes them into a tire and call it a good year.

ANDREW
Nice. I guess in your case, also an expensive year.

2. INT. SERIES TWO OPENING TITLES

3. INT. STAFF ROOM - DAY

We are in the hospital staff room located in the living room, it is the following morning. Chris and Jack, the two hospital surgeons are sat talking.

CHRIS
Well last night went fucking well.

JACK
Na, it didn't mate, I think that was the problem.

CHRIS
I pay good money and then they just take the piss out of me.

JACK
If all she can get out is piss you might want to see a doctor about that?

At this moment the hospitals resident doctor, Will Drew walks through the room.

WILL
Morning.

JACK

Why don't you just get yourself a girlfriend? Then you won't even have to pay?

      CHRIS
What? Like you do?

      JACK
Yes like me!

      CHRIS
And how is the Lord High Mrs Bitch Hypocrite today?

      JACK
It's actually just Lord High Hypocrite, The Mrs and Bitch made the name too long to fit in my phone contacts.

4. INT. HOSPTIAL KITCHEN - DAY

Now into the hospitals kitchen, stood looking out of the window is Andrew and the hospitals chef Biff Wellington.

We can see that they are looking out to the garden where the assistant manager Molly Hanson is sat talking to a patient.

      BIFF
I don't get why you just don't tell her you like her.

      ANDREW
Dignity my friend, dignity.

                    BIFF
Well nothing will ever happen if
you don't tell her, maybe get
Jack to give you a hand, a
double date sort of thing?

                    ANDREW
That might not be a bad idea.

Biff now picks up some roots from the side and throws them in a pan.

                    BIFF
Roots?

                    ANDREW
Oh I would.

                    BIFF
Sorry?

                    ANDREW
Er nothing. What was that about roots?

                    BIFF
From the veg, for the patients dinners.

                    ANDREW
Go ahead. It will be cheap.

5. INT. STAFF ROOM - DAY

Back into the staff room where Chris and Jack are still sat talking.

CHRIS
So what is the issue with you and her anyway?

JACK
Her.

CHRIS
And what does she say the issue is?

JACK
Me.

CHRIS
She's probably right.

At this moment the hospitals matron, Julia Walker walks into the room, armed with her usual box of bandages.

JULIA
Morning boys. I heard you had a bit of a problem last night Chris?

CHRIS
If you're going to suggest bandages as the cure, you can fuck off.

JULIA
Don't get dirty with me!

CHRIS
I wouldn't dream of it.. Well maybe in a nightmare.

JULIA
I was going to offer you help, just not like that.

CHRIS
Like what then?

JULIA
Well I'm always here to talk if you want advice in relationships.

JACK
I wouldn't exactly call it a relationship.

CHRIS
Yeah, but then again, a conversation with Julia, the last thing on my mind will be sex, let alone, bad sex.

JACK
Being a bit generous to yourself there mate, by the sounds of it, you didn't even manage sex.

At this moment there is the sound of a text being received from Jacks phone.

JACK (CONT'D)
Oh, it's from lord bitch…
        (he reads the text)
Do you want to meet up tonight?

At this second the door opens and Andrew walks in, he

grabs Jacks phone and replies to the text for him.

> ANDREW
> There, replied for you.

Jack looks at his phone again and reads the text out.

> JACK
> Yes babes, do you mind if I
> bring Andrew and Molly along?
> (he looks up at
> Andrew)
> Finally going to try get
> somewhere with her there?

> CHRIS
> Don't you mean somewhere up her?

> JACK
> Have you even asked her yet?

> CHRIS
> He's Aussie, they don't usually
> ask about those sorts of things.

6. INT. 10 SECOND BREAK UP SHOT #1

7. INT. HALLWAY - EVENING

It is early evening and we are in the hallway of the BHS Butterfield building. Waiting by the door is Jack and Andrew, dressed ready to go out for the evening.

> JACK
> (looking at his phone)
> She says she'll meet us there,

just Molly to wait for now.

Chris comes out of a door and walks up to them.

> CHRIS
> You wanted to see me?

> ANDREW
> Ah yeah, go something for you.

Andrew pulls something out of his pocket and hands it to Chris who sees its two bingo tickets.

> CHRIS
> Bingo Tickets?

> ANDREW
> Yeah.

> CHRIS
> Why is there two of them?

> JACK
> We didn't want you to be alone tonight.

> CHRIS
> Well who's my date?

Another door opens and out comes an old lady followed by Biff.

> BIFF
> (talking loudly)
> Here you go Miss Nichols, this is Christopher.

>   MISS NICHOLS
> I used to have a son called
> Christopher.
>
>   CHRIS
>   (turning to Jack and
>   Andrew)
> Your both wankers, I hope you
> know that.

At this moment Molly appears at the top of the stairs and walks down, she is also dressed ready to go out.

>   JACK
> Shit.
>
>   ANDREW
> Wow.

She reaches the bottom of the stairs, walks up to Andrew and kisses him on the cheek.

>   MOLLY
> Good Evening.

From another room.

>   JULIA (O.S.)
> If you're all planning on coming
> back and having fun tonight, can
> you please keep the noise down,
> I have a banging headache.... Oh
> and don't forget the protection.

8.   INT. RESTARUANT - EVENING

BHS Butterfield: The Complete First Series

We are in a classy restaurant full of people dressed up for the occasion.

Sat on a table for four is Andrew, Molly and Jack who is waiting for his girlfriend to arrive. A waiter walks up with the wine list and passes it to Molly.

>   WAITER
> Would madam care for some wine?

>   MOLLY
> May I Andrew?

>   ANDREW
> Of course, I'll buy you anything
> this evening.

>   MOLLY
>   (to waiter)
> This one please.

>   WAITER
> Certainly madam, that will be
> £15 a bottle.

>   MOLLY
> Thank y--

>   ANDREW
> Actually I don't seem to have
> that much money with me.

>   MOLLY
>   (to waiter)
> Glass of water please.

ANDREW
So, where is she?

At this moment, Jack's girlfriend, Louise walks in and up to the table.

JACK
Here she is.

Jack stands up to greet her and hug her however she ignores this and just sits down.

LOUISE
Sorry I'm late, just been with Jamie.

JACK
Jamie? Isn't that your ex?

LOUISE
Yeah, I saw him at lunch and just been catching up this afternoon.

JACK
I thought you were too busy to meet at lunch?

LOUISE
Yeah, with him. I hope you don't mind, only friends with him.

JACK
Didn't you once say he was an immature twat and that you never wanted to speak to him again

because he cheated on you, 3 times?

LOUISE
Yeah.

ANDREW
Sounds like you and him could have got on well.

Louise now turns her attention to Andrew.

LOUISE
Good evening.

ANDREW
Evening.

LOUISE
Well don't you look, and smell nice today...

ANDREW
Well don't you look and smell – shit today

She moves in close towards Andrew to smell his neck.

ANDREW (CONT'D)
Actually, I need the toilet, I'll be back in a minute.

Andrew leaves the table, in quite a hurry.

9. INT. MENS TOILET - MOMENTS LATER

Now in the men's toilet of the restaurant where Andrew walks in and starts to put his hands under the tab and wipe the sweat of his face. Jack walks in a few seconds later and does the same next to him.

> ANDREW
> She is a bitch mate.

> JACK
> Yeah, but I love her.

In the background the sound of two people moving inside a cubicle can be heard.

> ANDREW
> Seriously mate, I'm not sure she quite knows what a relationship is.

> JACK
> Yeah, but she is beautiful.

> ANDREW
> Don't worry, I'll start an optician's at the hospital next week to sort you out there.

The sound of people moving stops, following a few seconds of silence a cubicle door opens and Anthony Young, the hospitals original manager walks out and goes to wash his hands.

> ANTHONY
> Hi Jack.

> JACK

>   (looking confused)
>   Hi.

Anthony now walks out of the toilets.

>   ANDREW
>   Didn't I take his job?

At this point a woman in her mid-sixties walks out of the cubicle that Anthony previously came out of.

>   WOMAN
>   I can give you the same job if
>   you want my dear, only £30.

>   ANDREW
>   I think I feel sick.

>   JACK
>   Look on the upside mate... At
>   least at her age there wouldn't
>   be any teeth to dig in.

10. INT. BINGO HALL - EVENING

Now into a packed bingo hall, where sat at one of the tables are Chris and his date for the night, Mrs Nichols.

In the background is the noise of the bingo caller.

>   MRS NICHOLS
>   Well isn't this lovely dear.

>   CHRIS
>   Yes, would you like a drink Mrs
>   Nichols?

MRS NICHOLS
Sorry?

CHRIS
(slightly louder)
Would you like a drink?

MRS NICHOLS
Sorry my dear, I can't hear you?

CHRIS
(even louder, and
intimidating drinking)
Drink would you like?

MRS NICHOLS
Blowjob? Not yet my dear. Maybe later.

CHRIS
(shouting)
DRINK! NOT BLOWJOB!

Everyone in the room hears this and stops and stairs at him.

MRS NICHOLS
Sorry dear, what was that?

CHRIS
(to bingo caller)
Carry on.

BINGO CALLER
Naughty forty, number 40.

BHS Butterfield: The Complete First Series

CHRIS
I think I'd rather have one of them at the moment.

BINGO CALLER
Red Raw, 64.

MRS NICHOLS
Well I am one of them.

CHRIS
What 64?

MRS NICHOLS
No, red raw.

CHRIS
(after a delay)
I think I'm about to cut my own man hood off.

MRS NICHOLS
Well I'm into females to.

CHRIS
(after a delay)
I think I'm about to cut my own head off.

MRS NICHOLS
Well do be careful, it will make it sting down there dear.

CHRIS
I didn't mean that head.

> MRS NICHOLS
> Don't worry though, I can always kiss it better for you.

11. INT. 10 SECOND BREAK UP SHOT #2

12. INT. RESTARUANT - EVENING

Now back into the restaurant at the table where Molly and Louise have been talking when Andrew and Jack arrive back from the toilet and sit down.

As they sit, Jack goes to kiss Louise, however as he does Louise stands and walks over to Andrew to kiss him on the head, while Jack instead falls out of his seat onto the feet of the waitress that has just appeared.

> WAITRESS
> Your drinks.

> JACK
> (looking up)
> Thank-you.

> ANDREW
> When did we order?

> MOLLY
> While you were at the toilet, don't worry, I ordered your favourite, steak.

> LOUISE
> A big bit of meat for a real man.

JACK
What did you order me?

LOUISE
A smaller bit of meat.

JACK
Thanks.

The same woman that Jack and Andrew saw in the toilet appears at the table with plates of food.

WOMAN
Your food.

They all look up at the woman, Jack and Andrew both realize who it is.

ANDREW
I'm not so hungry.

JACK
Yeah, I feel the same.

WOMAN
Do you want any sauce with that... I make it myself.

13. EXT. OUTSIDE RESTARAUNT - MOMENTS LATER

Outside the restaurant, facing the door.

The door opens and Andrew followed by Jack and the two girls are walking out and down the street.

MOLLY

Why are we leaving so early?

> ANDREW
> Just fancied a walk instead.

> JACK
> Not so hungry after all, ate a lot of lunch, really nice today.

> ANDREW
> (to Jack)
> I'll be honest, that's never been said about biffs cooking before.

> JACK
> I don't think it ever will be again.

> LOUISE
> I fancy bed instead, with you in it.

> JACK
> Bit early isn't it?

> LOUISE
> I wasn't talking to you.

> JACK
> Right.

14. INT. HOSPITAL STAFF ROOM - EVENING

We are back at the hospital now in the staff room where

Julia is sat reading a magazine when Chris walks in and sits on one of the other sofas.

> JULIA
> You're back early.

> CHRIS
> Well I have been set up with a pensioner, she doesn't do late nights.

> JULIA
> Where is she now?

> CHRIS
> Toilet.

> JULIA
> Are you going to be getting any closer to her tonight?

> CHRIS
> Probably not.

> JULIA
> Why?

> CHRIS
> Because shes not my type.

> JULIA
> I didn't know you had a specific type?

> CHRIS
> Of course I do, I like them

young, free and single.

          JULIA
Well that second ones not entirely true.

          CHRIS
Okay, Young and under £100 a night.

          JULIA
Young? Are you getting pickier?

          CHRIS
I don't mind the occasional older one. They are cheaper after all.

          JULIA
Well I guess you have the sales of goods act to protect you with the quality. And I guess if they leak than you can get a refund.

          CHRIS
What do you mean leak?

          JULIA
It's a euphemism?

          CHRIS
No idea what you mean.

          JULIA
Are you saying you've never made a girl wet?

CHRIS
Is that what you're meant to do?

JULIA
Fuck me.... actually wrong phrase there, you don't sound very experienced at it.

CHRIS
Thanks.

JULIA
Maybe you should give this pensioner a go.

CHRIS
Why?

JULIA
She'll be experienced, can probably teach you a thing or two.

CHRIS
I would rather cut of my own penis and force feed it to myself.

JULIA
You don't need to offer to do that, I'm sure there are plenty of people who will do that for you... go on, give her a go.

CHRIS
No fucking way.

> JULIA
> Go on.

> CHRIS
> Go fuck yourself.

> JULIA
> I don't need to I have someone else to do that. Go on.

> CHRIS
> No.

> JULIA
> She only has a few weeks left to live and no one to give her inheritance to.

Chris stands up quickly and walks out the room.

> CHRIS
> Better find a bed.

15. EXT. PARK - EVENING

Now to a city centre park where we are looking at two benches next to each other, sat on one is Andrew with Molly at one side and Louise at the other, while Jack is sat alone on the other bench.

> LOUISE
> So Andrew, where are you from? You don't sound English.

> ANDREW
> Really? I thought my accent

sounded perfectly British.

                MOLLY
He's an Aussie.

                LOUISE
Oh, a criminal past, how sexy.

                ANDREW
I don't think you'd fit in there.

                LOUISE
Why not?

                ANDREW
The freaks are also across the ditch in New Zealand instead.

Louise's phone now rings.

                JACK
Who's that?

                LOUISE
Just Jamie, better answer it. It'll be about tomorrow, he's been texting me all night about it.

Louise answers her phone and walks out of shot. Andrew turns to Jack.

                ANDREW
Well mate, I can deffiently say, you have a complete bitch of a girlfriend there.

Molly grabs Andrew.

> MOLLY
> And you have me you Aussie criminal.

At this she moves in to kiss him without giving him any warning. Louise now comes back.

> JACK
> Sorted it with him?

> LOUISE
> Yeah, meeting him tomorrow.

> JACK
> I'm starting to see just why he always threatened to kill himself.

> LOUISE
> What do you mean?

> JACK
> Well you don't exactly treat your boyfriends well do you?

> LOUISE
> Fuck off.
> *(moving over to hug Andrew)*
> Hey Andrew.

At this point Molly breaks off the kiss with Andrew and slaps Louise in the face knocking her off the bench.

ANDREW

Thank-you Molly.

JACK

You've just slapped by girlfriend?

MOLLY

And I would again if it wasn't so busy.

ANDREW

Busy?

MOLLY

With you.

Molly grabs Andrew again and moves in for a second kiss.

16. INT. HOSPITAL CORRIDOR - EVENING

Back into the hospital in one of the corridors, where Biff is stood outside listening in on the room where Chris and Mrs Nichols are.

Julia walks up to Biff.

BIFF

Am I dreaming?

JULIA

Why?

BIFF

Because it sounds like Chris has actually got a woman who he is having sex with.

                JULIA
Is that really what you dream about?

After a short pause he answers.

                BIFF
No.

                JULIA
Right?

Julia now opens the door to the room.

                BIFF
What are you doing?

                JULIA
Well the woman he's got is a patient, needs her medication.

                BIFF
I must be dreaming, he's got someone in bed and you're working.

                JULIA
So you dream of Chris in bed and me doing jobs?

There is another pause.

                BIFF
Who's the patient anyway?

JULIA
Mrs Nichols.

BIFF
Hold on, isn't that --

JULIA
Yes, yes it is.

BIFF
Does he --

JULIA
No, no he doesn't.

BIFF
That's a laugh coming up then.

JULIA
Quite possibly.

At this Julia smiles and walks into the room.

17. EXT. PARK - EVENING

Back at the park benches. Andrew and Molly are sat on one still kissing each other and hugging while sat on the other is Jack and Louise, apart from each other.

LOUISE
You invite me along, then let your friend slap me.

JACK
In my defence, I didn't know she was going to do that.

                    LOUISE
You're meant to be protecting me.

Molly now takes a break from kissing Andrew and walks over to Jack and Louise. First she slaps Jack, Louise begins to laugh at this, before Molly turns to slap Louise as well.

                    MOLLY
            (to Louise)
    That's because you're a selfish
    bitch.
            (to Jack)
    That's because you invited her.

                    JACK
    You're in a real slapping mood
    today aren't you. Does Andrew not
    get one as well?

                    MOLLY
    I've got something else planned
    for him tonight.

                                        FADE TO BLACK.

18. INT. HALLWAY - MORNING

It is now the next morning and we are in the downstairs hallway of the hospital facing the closed kitchen door.

Julia appears and opens the door to find Biff stood there yawning with his hand down his trousers scratching.

                    JULIA
    Morning.

BIFF
Oh, Morning.

JULIA
Well I can say for certain your not dreaming right now.

BIFF
Why?

JULIA
Because if you were it wouldn't be your hand down there.

He quickly takes his hand out of his trousers and moves over to a pile of sandwiches, he passes one to Julia.

BIFF
Bacon.

JULIA
Well I hope it hasn't got any sausage in it.

BIFF
None, just bacon -- and meatball.

She picks a hair out of the sandwich.

JULIA
And pube.

BIFF
Hey, there a delicacy.

JULIA
Oh yeah, I forgot you've not
fully hit puberty yet.

19. INT. HOSPITAL STAFF ROOM - MOMENTS LATER

Now into the staff room where Jack is laid alone on one of the sofas.

Andrew walks into the room and sits on the other.

ANDREW
How did it go?

JACK
Well, could have been better.

ANDREW
Did you leave her?

JACK
Yep, both in relationship terms
and on the floor after Molly
slapped her -- again.

ANDREW
Yeah, she did seem really rough
last night. And she slapped her
quite a lot as well.

JACK
How did it go for you with
Molly?

ANDREW
Er, not bad. Bit soggy at

times.

> JACK
> Didn't need to know that bit.

> ANDREW
> Any idea how Chris did?

20. INT. BEDROOM - MORNING

We are now in one of the hospital bedrooms where laid in bed is Chris next to Mrs Nichols.

> MRS NICHOLS
> Well what a night, reminded me
> of what it was to be young.

> CHRIS
> I'm glad I could help.

> MRS NICHOLS
> Even the time reminded me, so
> quick.

There is a knock on the door.

> CHRIS
> Come in.

> MRS NICHOLS
> You can come in again if you
> want to love.

The door opens and the hospital mourner Adam Nichols walks in, he stops and stairs at the scene in front of him.

                    ADAM
Mother.

                    MRS NICHOLS
Oh, hello Adam.

                    CHRIS
What the fuck.

                    MRS NICHOLS
Do you want a go son?

                    CHRIS
On you or me?

                    MRS NICHOLS
Both.

                    ADAM
What?

                    CHRIS
I don't think he's into inbreeding, that's only Andrews family.

                    ADAM
And the French.

21. INT. STAFF ROOM - MOMENTS LATER

Back into the staff room where Jack is still laid and Andrew is talking to him.

The door bursts open and Chris walks in looking annoyed.

>CHRIS
>Why the fuck didn't you tell me
>that she was Adams mum.

>ANDREW
>Er, Jack will explain, I better
>get back to Molly.

With this Andrew quickly leaves the room.

>JACK
>Well...

There is a knock on the door.

22. EXT. OUTSIDE HOSPITAL - MOMENTS LATER

Outside the hospital facing the door we can see that it is Louise who is knocking, she knocks again.

The door opens and we see that it is Jack that answers.

>JACK
>I'd tap that If I was you, It's a
>very fragile door.

>LOUISE
>Well I'm a very fragile girl and
>you can tap me all you want.

>JACK
>Well I can't anymore can I?

>LOUISE
>You could always give me another
>Go?

JACK
With the amount of people you go for there might be quite a queue.

LOUISE
Come on give me another go.

JACK
Okay, I'll meet you later.

LOUISE
Where and when?

JACK
Come back here at seven.

23. INT. HALLWAY - CONTINUOUS

Now into the hall way where we see Jack close the door and turn round as Andrew walks into from another room holding a box of condoms.

JACK
Thought you were going back to Molly?

ANDREW
(holding the box up)
Needed to get some more of these.

JACK
Extra Large? Is that your cock or your head?

ANDREW
It's the head of my cock, I would show you but I might give you flashbacks to the last time you had sex with her.

JACK
Yep great. I can confirm that while she might be a bitch, she is female.

ANDREW
By the sounds of it, a lot of people can confirm that. What was that about anyway?

JACK
She wanted another go with me.

ANDREW
What did you say?

JACK
Meet me here at 7.

ANDREW
You can't be serious?

JACK
I am, but I have an idea.

ANDREW
What?

24. CLOSING TITLES

25. EXT. OUTSIDE HOSPITAL - EVENING

Back outside the hospital facing the front door where once again Louise is knocking and waiting for it to be answered.

The door opens, however it is Molly that is standing there. Without any talking she steps out and slaps Louise in the face knocking her over.

> MOLLY
> Hello.

Molly steps out of the way and we can see Andrew, Jack and Julia standing behind her.

> JACK
> Don't slap her too hard, I don't want her to end up a patient here.

> ANDREW
> That was your idea then?

> JACK
> Pretty much.

> ANDREW
> I must say, I like it mate.

> JULIA
> (to Louise)
> Do you need a bandage.

THE END

BHS Butterfield: The Complete First Series

Note from the Writer

The only issue which Angus had with the way the first series was written was that it did not include enough sex related or adult jokes and so this second series will include a lot more of them, as can be seen straight away in this episode, it makes up for the lack of those in the first series.

The main story of this episode is not focused within the hospital, but more with the relationships of the staff, particularly the relationship between Andrew and Molly, which throughout the first series there are hints of, particularly in the last episode.

I also felt that this episode needed some comical relationships put into it as well, after all, BHS Butterfield is a comedy show, so it was only natural to use the two surgeons for this.

Louise is Jack's girlfriend in this episode. The first two episodes for series two are not yet written but it is planned for her to be introduced in one of these. While she may seem a minor character, appearing in at most 2 or 3 episodes when the second series is completely written, she is the character that is causing the most controversy, while there is a long and comical story to this, now is not the time to talk about it.

BHS Butterfield: The Complete First Series

Behind the Ideas

So that's it for the screenplays, I hope you enjoyed reading them, they took a while to write and much much longer to format for this book.

This next section of the book will tell you a bit more about the ideas behind the sitcom and what the initial plans were.

Originally, the intention was for myself and Angus to produce the show ourselves and release the first series on You Tube to see what people thought of it, we also planned to set up a You Tube partnership and make a financial return on the work we put it which would have also helped fund a second series if necessary. Following that we were going to submit commissioning proposals to various production companies and TV channels both in the UK and abroad, the responses from the first You Tube released series would have been used as part of the proposal.

In the end, we had to cancel our production of the first series, there is two reasons for this. The first reason is that we had a major issue in terms of lack of location, Angus was the location manager, one of the few off screen roles that he had, and despite for months assuring me that he would have a location sorted well before the intended filming dates, he found this job to be a lot harder than he first anticipated when he agreed to take it up. The second reason was due to a number of last minute drop outs from cast who originally agreed to participate in the production.

There were many, many people who said that we would never ever get anywhere with it and that it would never be successful, all I can ever say to these people is why? How do you know that? The truth of it is, we did fail without intended original production, as the executive producer of that production project, it is left to me to take responsibility for it being cancelled, and I do, however there were a number of things that were

BHS Butterfield: The Complete First Series

not down to me that led to its overall cancellation.

So we did fail with the initial production, but that doesn't mean that we have failed with BHS Butterfield, after all, right now you are reading it as a book, it's just a different approach to it.

The only people who can make a project fail are those which think it can fail, and that is what led to the cast drop outs and overall us having to cancel production. However there may well be a time when instead of reading BHS Butterfield you are able to watch it on TV as a sitcom as it was intended to be.

If there is one message you take away after reading this book, a serious message, it would be to always try and keep going if you think that you are onto something, and by that I mean YOU think that, in no way does it matter what someone else, or a thousand other people think, if you think you have a good idea go for it, if someone thinks you will fail then prove them wrong. Forget about how old or how young you are, at the end of the day, age does not determine success, if you have written a book, get out and sell it, if you want to be on TV, contact some agents, just remember to trust yourself and ignore the rest. If you are still at school and have an idea, don't wait until you get older, a young person's approach can be something which leads to success and there is no reason why you should wait, or why you cannot do it now, anything is possible when you put your mind to it, life takes place in a big world, not one small school, so make the most of it, get out there, live life and do not let anything get in your way.

That's enough of the deep messages anyway. It's time to tell you how I and Angus got the idea for BHS Butterfield.

We first came up with the initial idea to create a comedy show back in January 2011 when we were sat in a photography lesson, as was often common in these lessons, we were not really doing a large amount of work, photography lessons were always some of the more relaxed in the school week, in fact to give you an idea of just how laid back these lessons (and our teacher) were, we spent an entire weeks lessons planning out the teachers wedding, then deciding that one of the students would be the vicar for the wedding and doubling up as the emergency husband-to-be if required.

Anyway, back to the point. Me and Angus used to spend these lessons talking about and discussing many different things, including just how annoying one particular fellow student was, and how funny another one was (unintentionally), however it was this January when we first came up with the idea to create a comedy show, over Christmas the BBC started to screen the first series of the mockumentary show 'Come Fly With Me' (for non UK viewers who have no idea what this show is, you are missing out). This show inspired us, and we decided that we would create our own sketch mockumentary show, as you do.

For those of you unsure what the term mockumentary is, in short it's a genre of comedy show which follows the format of a documentary but is fictional and written in a way which often over exaggerates events or simply takes the piss out of the subject of the 'documentary', in 'Come Fly with Me' this is the aviation industry. To begin with, we tried many different ideas, including basing it in a school where the male headteacher would begin each day by standing at the school gates sending home any girls who have too short a skirt on but then sending home any female teacher who has a too long a skirt on.

It turns out however that although myself and Angus do have direct experience of a school, and recent experience of one, seen as though we were still there at this time, setting a mockumentary in this sort of environment was not that easy to write. There has of course been other comedy shows set in schools, notably 'Bad Education' and 'Big School' and both of these shows do work well, however I do think that to write a mockumentary for a school setting, it would require more comedy and writing experience than I had at the time, and so we looked for other ideas.

It was soon after this that we hit on what we considered to be comedy gold (open to debate and opinion, but do read all of this book first), we decided to base our show in a hospital, a setting which we felt there would be no shortage of comedy, and so we came up with some initial sketches mostly involving the two surgeons who were the first character to be developed and a useless manager character who later became Anthony Young in the series.

When writing the initial pilot screenplay, I began to think that it would work much better as a sitcom rather than a mockumentary come sketch show, so I instead wrote a sitcom pilot screenplay for the concept, using many of the initial sketches from the mockumentary pilot one but with more development. Angus agreed with my thinking on this and that is how the idea for a hospital based sitcom came about, as it would allow me to develop characters, relationships between them and plot lines much further throughout individual episodes, series and the show as a whole. Right now, you may be asking yourself why we called the show BHS Butterfield, or you might even be asking yourself, how do I contact the creators of this brilliant comedy show to ask them why they called it BHS Butterfield, or most likely, you will be asking yourself, Do I really care why they called it BHS Butterfield and what do I fancy for dinner, well the answer to that last question would yes you do care and you fancy bacon for dinner, bacon is always a good option for food no matter what the time of day, unless your vegetarian in which case have a leaf.

Regardless of whether you care or not, I am going to be telling you why we did actually call it BHS Butterfield. The name of the hospital in the show is BHS Butterfield, and therefore that became the name of the actual show.

BHS Butterfield: The Complete First Series

The second part of the name has had no imagination or creativity put into it, we simply used Butterfield because we could not think of a better name and just ended up deciding to use the name of one of the creators, that and Butterfield has a much better ring to it than my name does, plus it does sound like it could be a real hospital too.

The BHS bit of the name has much more of a story to it. In the show it stands for 'British Health Service', despite it being a private hospital. We did originally want to use the name NHS Butterfield, which is probably the name which you would expect us to have used. Annoyingly it does turn out however that 'NHS' is a registered trademark belonging to the Department for Health and we needed permission of them to use it.

We did attempt to get permission from them, and surprisingly to begin with, they did not seem to have any issue with us using it, that was right up until the point when they asked to see one of the screenplays and they found out that what we were doing was mocking them and their operations and showing them in a bad light. This was when they said no and banned us from using the name NHS, the term NHS within the show and the use of any NHS published material and stuff like that in the show.

Personally, I do not think that this was very fair of them, after all, the NHS is a public service that just happens to be owned and paid for by the taxpayer, a group of people which myself, Angus and most likely you the reader are a part of, so surely then, I should be allowed to use the name of something which technically I do own a part of? I did reason this with them, but they, as you can probably tell, did not agree with my point.

You may have noticed that each of the episodes you read were around 23 pages (in A4 anyway) long, this is something for which there is a simple answer to. If the show was commissioned by a TV channel, we would have to keep to the technical requirements for

BHS Butterfield: The Complete First Series

than channel, and as many show adverts, this would mean a show length of 23 minutes per half hour scheduled slot.

One question which I do often get asked is how to go about actually writing a sitcom, I feel that any writer will have a different answer to this, often sitcom writers are comedians, I see myself and Angus more as comedians than authors, and I think that this can help to create a sitcom.

Quite often, the material written into a sitcom is the same or similar to that which the writer will include in their stand up performances. For example, 'Not Going Out' written by Lee Mack has many many jokes from Lee's stand up written into it, although they are often developed to fit into the show.

When it came to writing BHS Butterfield, I started by coming up with basic possible story lines for each episode, I sent these to Angus and between us we narrowed it down to the ones that would be used to create an episode.

From this, I knew which story would be used for each episode and went on to decide where the episode would begin and where it would end, this would also be moulded around fitting the episodes together after series long plot lines were decided upon.

For the opening scenes before the title sequence I wanted something which was immediately comical on its own, on a couple of occasions this is the two surgeons talking to each other and on others it is other hospital staff with taking the piss out of the surgeons, as in 'A Day for Love' which has what I feel the best opening sequence that I have written.

The next part of writing the episode is deciding upon certain jokes that I wanted to include in the episode, I then write a scene that is around this joke, these scenes on their own however do not form an overall story and when writing the scenes that link them together to form the episode, changes are made so that the overall story of the episode flows throughout.

The scenes that link scenes together are the last to be written and often follow the story line for that episode the most, if the previous scene goes off the plot then the linking one will bring it back.

Time for a quick rant. I am sure that every student will have had at some point a teacher that will read something and state the writer wrote something in a certain way to show a certain thing, well, most of the time, and particularly in the case of BHS Butterfield, this is a load of shit. Likewise, a Media teacher thinks that characters or particular plots are written in order to show something or represent a group of people, this is also mostly just bollocks, in BHS Butterfield and many other sitcoms and shows, they are written to be entertaining or funny, not for representation. I have written BHS Butterfield as a sitcom to be comical and entertain an audience, not to be dissected by English and Media teachers.

BHS Butterfield: The Complete First Series

Future Plans for BHS Butterfield

As you may have already noticed, there is a series two episode included in this book, that does of course mean that I was intending to write a second series. While I have only written the one episode for this second series, I do have basic plans for each episode.

Series Two – Episode One – Recruitment Drive

In the second series I wanted to have a few new cast, this meant that I would have to write out some of the old characters and write in a few new ones into the series. So I decided that the first episode of series two could show just this, with Andrew interviewing new candidates for a number of roles, including a new doctor, with the help of the two surgeons, all three taking their usual approach to work.

While I never fully planned out which characters would be written out and who the new ones would be, I can confirm that Andrew, Molly, Chris, Jack, Adam, Biff, Julia and Anthony would all be staying for the second series.

Series Two – Episode Two – The New Ambulance

By the second series we were intending to have an actual budget, and so we wanted to get an ambulance for the hospital after the bike and staff cars they use break down.

In this episode Chris and Jack have to travel out to a British coastal town to rescue some surfers and bring them back to the hospital for urgent treatment, however due to their car breaking down, they have to do this on public transport.

Series Two – Episode Four – Sex Clinic

BHS Butterfield: The Complete First Series

In this episode Andrew gives Chris and Jack the job of creating a new service at the hospital by introducing a sex clinic, they of course do this in their usual fashion.

Series Two – Episode Five – Return of the Kiwi

As the episode title suggests, there would be a return of Andrews New Zealand cousin in this episode, I am also quite interested in introducing a second member of his family, possibly a sibling or a parent if it could be fitted into the series.

Series Two – Episode Six – Royal Visit

This would be the series closer but also the show closer, that is right, after this episode I has no intentions to write a third series, although there were some plans after this.

To close it off, I wanted to go big, the idea for this episode came to me in the first week of last September, living in Doncaster, this is of course the week of the St Ledger Festival, and while the royal family are not known for attending this event, they are well known for attending other horse racing events.

This episode would begin by showing the royal family at a horse race meeting when one of them falls ill or injures themselves, of course they have to come to BHS Butterfield with the usual bunch of staff there to help them out.

BHS Butterfield – Down Under

Myself and Angus thought that there was potential for BHS Butterfield to be a feature presentation as well as a TV sitcom. And that's how we came up with the idea of 'BHS Butterfield- Down Under', in short Andrew is going home and taking a few staff with him.

BHS Butterfield: The Complete First Series

What we get Asked

Since the initial release of BHS Butterfield as an e-book we have been asked many questions regarding the series and so we want to take the opportunity to answer a few of them in this latest edition. So here we go.

Who are you comedy influences?

Certainly for me writing the series one of the big influences is Lee Mack and his show 'Not Going Out', however there are also many other both UK and international comedians which I use for inspiration and are an influence on my writing of the series, this includes Andrew Hansen, who as I have said before is the person the character of Andrew Harris is based upon, however comedians such as Dai Henwood, Jeremy Corbett, Paul Ego, Tim Vine and Hugh Dennis, all of which have done TV work, some have written sitcoms are influences.

For Angus, he is influenced from more old classical comedy and series such as 'Monty Python', often many of the discussions we had when creating the series involved sending links to clips from the show on You Tube and seeing what ideas we could create from it.

Do you think that you went too far in some episodes?

I think that this is down to individual judgment and will vary between each person who reads the series, what I can say though is that neither myself or Angus think that we went too far in what we created.

We do however know that in some episodes, such as 'Inspection Day' we went really far with some of the jokes and we may have offended some people, but I do think that this is just the nature of writing comedy, to stand out you have to push the boundaries of political correctness and not be afraid to go to the limit of what may be considered too far.

Of course it is difficult to know what is too far, as this will vary from demographic to demographic, this book is being released in a lot of different countries and each of those will result in a different reaction to what we have created.

In relation to the Germans in episode two however, while we did go much further than John Cleese ever did, the German scenes from Fawlty Towers are some of the most memorable comedy scenes ever written.

Is writing a screenplay harder than writing a story?

In my personal opinion it is much much harder. The reason for this is because there is a big difference between a screenplay and a story, a story tells the story directly to the audience, where as a screenplay tells the cast and crew hot to tell the story to the audience.

With BHS Butterfield, as myself and Angus were originally intending to produce the show ourselves, we knew how each scene was going to be filmed and directed and so I did not need to put loads of detail into the script, we also wanted a degree of improvisation from the cast to really make the character they were portraying their own.

Other screenplay's which I have written or are in the process of writing do have much more detail regarding production in them than the BHS Butterfield series does, simply because they are not ones that I intend to produce myself.

There is a challenge in writing a script in the way you want other people to produce it as every director and every production team will have their own way of doing it. I think it would be quite interesting to see how a different director and production team would produce BHS Butterfield, they might see it in the same way as myself and Angus did and take the same approach to production as we would, or alternatively they might see it in a completely different way and go on to produce it in such a way.

Are your school in support of the book?

Mostly is the short answer to this question. In truth, most teachers and school staff did not actually know about the book or the series to begin with. Around a month after the initial e-book release we appeared in a local paper under the title 'Pairs sitcom is social media hit', it was this that made school notice the book.

I was quite surprised, as was Angus just how many teachers read that paper, for the next few days every teacher we spoke to mentioned it to us, our head of sixth form however seemed rather annoyed at me to begin with, all because we did not have our top buttons done up in the photo, personally I think that there was a much worse issue with the photo we used, this being that it was taken against a background of brick wall, and it was rather obvious it was not taken completely straight.

There has been a generally good response from our teachers, one in particular who is eager to read the book as his wife works in the NHS, he also gave suggestions for the series that were in fact more offensive than the ones we came up with ourselves. The Rugby coaching team have also asked about the series and seem quite interested, probably because I have missed a few training sessions as I've been busy promoting.

However, there is one particular member of school staff who seems to be very much against the book, and also more recently against myself, I think this is somewhat due to a complaint she could not do anything about though.

Do you and Angus see yourselves as writers or comedians?

BHS Butterfield: The Complete First Series

Angus cannot call himself a writer as he has not actually written any of the series and his only writing contribution to this book was his short introduction at the beginning of the book.

I see myself as a writer and a comedian. I have written other screenplay's not just comedy, however in terms of BHS Butterfield and other comedy projects I am working on, I do see myself as a comedian. I will never see myself as an author though as I am not a story writer but I do see myself as a screenwriter.

I think it would also be accurate to say that authors spend quite a lot of time reading as well as writing, this is certainly not true for me, in the past two years I have only read two books, one of these is the All Black captains Richie McCaw's autobiography and the other is titled 'Bucket list of an idiot' by Dom Harvey, on a side note both are good reads.

I consider Angus to be a comedian, as he does create comedy as do I, other people may not agree with that and it is up to them how they see us, but I'd like to think that they find what we have created to be funny and they see us as comedians. After all, a comedian does not have to write stand up.

Is it harder to write or promote the book?

Promote by a long way. Writing the book did take a long time, and the formatting and proofing even longer, however as I am starting to find out, promoting is a full time and very stressful job. The promotion is also made harder as I am trying to promote a book which should actually be a sitcom on TV.

Angus is taking his usual approach and leaving the promotion mostly to me, he tends not to mind too much what I do so long as it gets more sales. So, what am I doing? Well apart from getting little sleep and starting at a computer for too long (no need to be dirty minded there) I am talking to various radio and TV producers and presenters from around the world trying to get promotion as well as advertising on social media websites such as Twitter and Facebook.

Why do some scenes seem cheap to produce?

By this question, I can only presume that people are referring to the scenes such as the outdoor consulting area. In short they are meant to be cheap to produce, partly to help keep a low production budget and partly to fit with the idea that the hospital is cheap.

BHS Butterfield: The Complete First Series

The Conclusion

I am afraid that we have now come to the end of the book, almost (still these last few pages to go), I can only hope that you did enjoy what you read, if you did then why not tell your friends and family to buy the book as well? We will love you for it. Please also remember that while BHS Butterfield might not be the most expertly written sitcom in the world, neither myself or Angus have has any professional experience before this.

Neither of us have any idea where this will take us, it might end up being a complete failure, or it might actually be a success, we are hoping for the later, feel free to disagree with me there.

One quick rant before I end this book. Just before I wrote this section, I was talking to Angus on Facebook regarding book promotion, hurray for us, if you are reading this, our promoting is somewhat working.

I clicked onto my homepage thing and my news feed is, as usual full of all sorts of crap, life stories of those I do not know, adverts for hoovers, the occasional naked person (I have told Angus not to post those photos) and all that, however there was one thing that caught my eye, relating to the American sitcom 'Big Bang Theory', I have never watched the show, my ex used to try get me to watch it and I just refused, call me weird if you want, but I want to rant about what I saw, this picture said that to make the perfect sitcom you need a characters that is the 'nerd' and the 'cute one' etc. Now, to the person who created that picture and all those who agree with it, try actually writing a sitcom, they are meant to be original, not follow some strict convention, they are not easy to write or come up with ideas for, but that does not mean follow the same character set out as some other show.

If you want to know what I mean by hard, then try it (that also happens to be Angus's favourite chat up line), comedy alone is hard to

BHS Butterfield: The Complete First Series

write but fitting that comedy into a situation and creating the characters for it is difficult, really difficult, and as stupid as some comedians may seem, for example, Lee Mack, for him to create a show as successful as 'Not Going Out', he has to be an intelligent guy.

So that is the end and all from me for now. To you the reader, cheers for buying, hope you enjoyed it.

E noho rā

BHS Butterfield: The Complete First Series

About the Creators

BHS Butterfield: The Complete First Series

Angus Butterfield

Born as Charles 'Angus' Saxon Butterfield on December 10th 1995 in Doncaster, South Yorkshire where he continues to have lived since birth. At the time of publication Angus is aged 17.

He has previously had one appearance on TV in the U.S, briefly appearing in a clip shown on MTV's Ridiculousness show, which has also screened in the UK on a number of occasions. Although the clip was not great quality and you cannot actually tell that it is him in the 6 second clip, he did get paid for it, and it does count as a TV appearance. This clip of Angus attempting to spear himself with a Javelin very nearly also appeared on 'Harry and Paul's Magnificent Sporting Moments', but despite also being paid for this production, he didn't quite make the final cut of the show.

Angus is known to be ridiculously gullible with females, this was first demonstrated on a trip to a politics conference in December 2012 at Hull University, when on the way to the student union to buy some lunch, Angus was stopped by three female cheerleaders who convinced him to buy a number of raffle tickets for a student only prize draw that he was not eligible for. Further evidence for this theory on Angus came about in summer 2013 when walking through his local town a saleswoman managed to sell him some very feminine make-up for which he has no use for.

As a keen businessman, Angus have developed a wide knowledge of business in a general sense and through working on various ideas with Ben, more specific knowledge on particular industries, with much focus on the aviation industry.

From a young age he has had an interest into the workings of the aviation industry and if it ever came to it, he could probably fly a

BHS Butterfield: The Complete First Series

Boeing 747 on a full flight, so long as nothing drastic and navigation was not a priority that is.

On top of core subjects, Angus also has GCSE's in the subjects of Classics, Geography, Geology and Photography. For sixth form study he chose the options of Classics, Physics and Geography and hopes to study geological engineering at university level in either Manchester or London.

Outside of School, Angus has a keen interest in athletics and Javelin for which he trains 2-3 times a week, as well as spending his spare time longboarding and breaking things along with his friends. He also has a keen interest in skiing and never turns down the chance to visit X-scape.

Part of the band 'Fleet of Men', Angus is also a keen guitarist and has performed along with the band live at a number of small local venues.

When initially planning the production of BHS Butterfield, Angus was cast in the role of Chris Lister which was specifically written around his personality and would have also acted as one of the show's producers.

His contribution to the show was helping to develop the initial idea into a working concept and reviewing what Ben wrote.

Follow Angus on Twitter

@Jewbacca_o

BHS Butterfield: The Complete First Series

Ben Wagstaff

Born February 16th 1996 in Chelmsford, Essex before moving at a very young age to Huntingdon, Cambridgeshire and then later to Doncaster, South Yorkshire when his mother left the family.

Ben is a trained radio presenter and producer however he has only ever got round to producing the one solo show due to many other commitments and a lack of free time.

A keen supporter of the All Blacks, Wellington Hurricanes in Super Rugby and Taranaki in the ITM, he often got a lot of stick for wearing a Taranaki shirt during training for the sport at school as one of the coaches was from Auckland, New Zealand.

In November 2012 however he did run into the Maori All Blacks while walking through town after training, which became only the second time anyone in Doncaster recognised the Taranaki shirt, with three of the players, Andre Taylor, Jamison Gibson Park and former All Black Jarred Hoeata all congratulating him on his shirt choice. A similar experience happened later that week at the Maori All Black v Champion Select XV match where a number of the Maori players from the Wellington Hurricanes shook his hand before the match congratulating him for his choice of Hurricanes shirt.

For comedic influence Ben looks up to comedians such as Lee Mack and Rowan Atkinson and looks to the work of writers such as Ben Elton when it comes to writing the screenplays and Dom Harvey for the non-screenplay writing.

Ben spends much of his spare time travelling and developing new ideas for either screenwriting or business.

BHS Butterfield: The Complete First Series

In February 2014 he intends to launch a new investment business within the media industry which will aim to launch the careers of other people. He hopes to work on this business into the future to grow and develop it further.

Ben obtained GCSE's in all core subjects and also in Drama, History, Photography and Geography. He has also studied English Language, Economics, Politics and Media at AS, all of which but the later were continued into A2 studies.

When initially planning the series production Ben was cast in the series and would have acted as the show's Executive Producer and Director among a range of many other crew roles both on and off set throughout all stages of production.

Also, as writer of the book you are currently reading, Ben is now a published writer.

Follow Ben on Twitter

@Ben_Wagstaff

BHS Butterfield: The Complete First Series

BHS Butterfield: The Complete First Series

bhsbutterfield.com

info@bhsbutterfield.com

Follow BHS Butterfield on Twitter

@BHS_Butterfield

#BHSButterfield

Find BHS Butterfield on Facebook

BHSButterfieldBook

Follow Ben on Twitter

@Ben_Wagstaff

Follow Angus on Twitter

@Jewbacca_o

Made in the USA
Charleston, SC
01 December 2013